Britain and the Great War

J F AYLETT

Hodder & Stoughton

LONDON SYDNEY AUCKLAND

ACKNOWLEDGEMENTS

The publishers would like to thank the following for permission to reproduce copyright illustrations in this volume:

Reproduced by permission of The Imperial War Museum p4 right; p8 left; p8 right; p9; p10 left; p14 left;. p14 right; p21 left; p22 top right; p24; p25 left; p28 left; p31 left; p32 left; p34 left; p35 left; p35 right; p37; p39 right; p40; p41 left; p56 left; p58 left; p62 left.
T & V Holt Associates p6 right; p15 top; p24 left; p26 left; p 26 right; p27; p34 right; p36 right; p42; p44 left; p44 right; p46 right; p49 left; p52 left; p53; p54 left; p60 left; p61.
Topham Picture Source p7 right; p30; p60 right.
Courtesy of the Director, National Army Museum, London p11, p16.
Musee de l'Armee, Paris: Francois Flameng- "Eglise d'Albert, Somme, 5 aout, 1916" p5 left; "Notre-Dame-de-Lorette, 28 juin 1915" p12 top; "Guetteurs Allemands, aout, 1917" p19 right.
Liddle Collection, Leeds University Library p13; p29 left; p31 right; p47 right.
Collection Albert Kahn- cover; p15 middle; p18 left; p18 right; p22 left; p33; p38; p63.
Collection Viollet p15 lower.
The British Library, Newspaper Collection p20 left
The Hulton-Deutsch Picture Company p28 right; p46 left; p55 left; p59 right.
Popperfoto p22 bottom right; p41 right.
Reproduced by permission of the Trustees of the Rupert Brooke Estate/ King's College Library , Cambridge p43.
John Frost Newspaper Library p45 top; p52 right; p59 left.
David Evans p50 right; p51.
The National Museum of Labour History p55 right.
The National Library of Ireland p56 right.
Office of Public Works, Kilmainham Gaol, Dublin p57.

The publishers would also like to thank the following for permission to reproduce copyright material:

Edward Arnold (Publishers) Limited for the extracts from *The Great War* by David Evans (1981) and *Britain and the Great War* by JM Bourne (1989); Oxford University Press for the extracts from *The Great War and Modern Memory* by Paul Fussell (1975) and *Echoes of the Great War, the Diary of the Reverend Andrew Clark 1914-1918* by James Munson (1985); Samson Books Ltd for the extract from *Twice in a Lifetime* by Leslie Walkington (1980); AP Watt Ltd on behalf of the Robert Graves Copyright Trust for the extract from *Goodbye To All That* by Robert Graves; Cassell PLC for the extract from *Cannon Fodder* by A Stuart Dolden; Alan Sutton Publishing for the extract from *The Western Front Illustrated* by John Laffin (1991); Penguin Books Ltd for the extracts from *Voices and Images of the Great War 1914-1918* by Lyn Macdonald c Lyn Macdonald (1991), first published by Michael Joseph Ltd (1988) and for the extracts from *An Illustrated Companion to the First World War* by Anthony Bruce (Michael Joseph 1989) c Anthony Bruce 1989; Francis Day & Hunter Ltd London for the songs 'Belgium Put the Kibosh on the Kaiser' words and music by A Ellerton 1914 and 'Goodbye-ee' words and music by RP Weston and Bert Lee 1917; Batsford for the extracts from *Christmas Cards for the Collector* by Arthur Blair, *Growing Up in the First World War* by Renee Huggett and *The Great War* by Richard Tames; Longman Group UK for the extracts from *The Home Front* by Sarah Davies, *World War I* by Dudley Woodget and *The Western Front* by Peter Liddle; Routledge for the extract from *The Great War 1914-1918* by Marc Ferro; Chatto & Windus for the extract from *A Cab at the Door* by VS Pritchett ; Multer (Frederick) for the extract from *Daily Sketches* by Martin Walker (1978); Rogers, Coleridge & White Ltd for the extract from *Akenfield* by Ronald Blythe; David & Charles Publishers, Newton Abbott, England for the extract from *People At War* by Michael Moynihan (1973); Daily Mail/Solo Syndication for the report dated 17 April 1916; American Heritage, a division of Forbes Inc for the extracts from *The American Heritage History of World War I* by SLA Marshall c1985; Heinemann Educational Books Ltd for the extract from *The First World War* by Nigel Kelly; Jonathan Cape for the extract from *Voices From The Great War* by Peter Vansittart; Ascherberg Hopwood & Crew/Warner Chappell Music Ltd for the song 'Keep The Home Fires Burning' 1914; William Heinemann Ltd (incorporating Peter Davies) for the extract from *My Warrior Sons* by Guy Slater; Random House for the extract from *Trench Fighting* by Charles Messenger; Sidgwick & Jackson for the extracts from *The Imperial War Museum Book of the First World War* by Malcolm Brown.

Illustrations by Gay Galsworthy

British Library Cataloguing in Publication Data

Aylett, J. F.
  Britain and the Great War. – (Past Historic Series)
  I. Title II. Series
  941.083

  ISBN 0 340 58363-0

First published 1993
Impression number 10 9 8 7 6 5 4 3 2 1
Year   1998   1997 1996 1995 1994 1993

© 1993 J. F. Aylett

Typeset by Litho Link Ltd, Welshpool, Powys, Wales
Printed in Great Britain for the educational publishing division of Hodder & Stoughton Ltd, Mill Road, Dunton Green, Sevenoaks, Kent by Scotprint Ltd, Musselburgh

CONTENTS

1	A Word about Propaganda	4
2	Countdown to War	6
3	Off to War	8
4	Trench Warfare	10
5	Stalemate	16
6	Weapons Old and New	18
7	The Battle of the Somme	20
8	Attitudes Change	22
9	From Volunteers to Conscripts	24
10	Singing Through the Shelling	26
11	On the Home Front	28
12	War in the Air	36
13	More New Technology	38
14	The Third Battle of Ypres	40
15	The War in Poetry	42
16	The War at Sea	44
17	1918	46
18	How Attitudes Changed	52
19	Change in Politics	54
20	Ireland	56
21	The Treaty of Versailles	58
22	Britain after the War	60
23	Change and Continuity	62
	Glossary	64
	Index	65

No one knows exactly how many people died in the Great War. We never will. Even today, more remains are found each year in France or Belgium. Farmland is still littered with the débris of a war which ended over 70 years ago.

No one can be certain how much it all cost, either. But Britain alone was spending over £6 million a day by spring 1918. By the standards of the time, that was a massive amount of money. Historians have estimated that, on average, it cost £8,000 to kill a man in the Great War.

Of course, in 1914, few thought about dying. Young men from all over Europe could hardly wait to go and fight: war was seen as heroic, romantic and a great adventure. The reality was one of the worst events that human beings have ever devised. This book is the story of that event.

A WORD ABOUT PROPAGANDA

One of the first casualties in any war is the truth. In 1914, the British government wanted men to fight Germany; at the same time, it wanted neutral countries to stay friendly to Britain. To do this, it used propaganda.

Propaganda means a plan to spread ideas and beliefs. Its aim is to get everyone to accept these ideas, whether they are true or not. There are various ways of doing this. One is to censor the news so that bad news is not published. Another is to spread rumours. A third way is to spread downright lies.

The British government did all these things during the Great War. Newspapers went along with this. The Germans were called 'Huns' – the name of a barbarian tribe in the 5th century AD. Other names they used were 'vandals' or 'blond brutes'.

The government wanted people to believe that the Germans were cruel and evil. There were newspaper reports that they crucified enemy soldiers; they raped nuns; they bayoneted babies. Cartoons, like this one by a Dutchman, helped to keep the rumours going.

One of the rumours was about Russian soldiers who landed in Scotland to fight with the British. The story spread like wildfire. It was supposed to have been started by a railway porter who asked some Scottish soldiers where they had come from. They replied, 'Ross-shire' but he thought they said 'Russia'. In fact, the Secret Service spread the story to raise morale and mislead the enemy.

The propaganda did not stop at rumours. Everywhere, there were posters urging men to join the army. But posters had another aim: they made people believe it was right to hate the Germans. This is just one example:

Newspaper reports were censored and reporters were not allowed into front-line trenches until late in the war. So most of the news was propaganda: losses were given as gains; defeats were written up as victories.

The soldiers themselves learned not to believe the newspapers. They put their trust in what other soldiers told them. As a result, rumours became one of the war's deadly weapons.

Over 20 years later, Germany would use the same techniques in the Second World War. Its propaganda chief said he learned everything from what the British did in the Great War.

F *The Times* news item of April 1917. It claims that a German newspaper reporter

. . . published last Tuesday the first German admission concerning the way in which the Germans use dead bodies. He writes:

'We pass through Evernigcourt. There is a dull smell in the air, as if lime were being burnt. We are passing the great Corpse Exploitation Establishment (*Kadaververwertungsanstalt*) of this Army Group. The fat is turned into lubricating oils. Everything else is ground down into a powder which is used for mixing with pigs' food and as manure.'

G As source E.

No one knows who it was who [made up] the German Corpse Works. This legend held that fats were so scarce in Germany that battlefield corpses were taken back by the Germans to [be turned into fats]. The legend probably [started] in an intentional British mistranslation of the phrase *Kadaver Anstalt* on a captured German order – in German, animal remains.

Most of the sources on these pages are propaganda. In two cases, the authors did not know they were writing propaganda because the rumours had become so common. Despite this, a historian can learn much from these sources. They show us what people believed during the war and from them we can work out what their attitude was towards the Germans.

C A painting of the church at Albert (1915). A German shell had damaged the statue of the Virgin.

The 'leaning Virgin' became a landmark for British troops. It seemed almost a miracle that it had not fallen. In fact, the Royal Engineers kept it in position. In March 1918, the tower was demolished. The British were told that the Germans had shot it down. The truth is that the British destroyed it to stop the Germans using it as an observation post.

D David Evans: *The Great War* (1981).
A British Expeditionary Force under Sir John French crossed the Channel. Together with their French allies, [they] moved into Belgium to meet the advancing Germans. The men of the BEF [were] referred to by the Kaiser as 'a contemptible little army'.

E Paul Fussell: *The Great War and Modern Memory* (1975).
The Kaiser, it was said, had referred to the British troops as 'a contemptible little army.' It is now known that the phrase [came] not from the German side but from British propagandists, who needed something memorable to [inspire] the troops. The phrase was actually devised at the War Office by Sir Frederick Maurice.

1 a) What is propaganda?
   b) What idea of the Germans do you get in
   (i) source A and (ii) source B?
   c) Why did the artists want people to have these ideas?
   d) Explain what we can learn from (i) source B and (ii) source C.
2 a) How do sources D and E disagree?
   b) Which do you believe? Give reasons.
   c) If source E is correct, why would the War Office want people to think the Kaiser said this? (Give more than one reason.)
3 a) Read sources F and G. What did *The Times* want people to think was happening?
   b) Does the German reporter say that human corpses were being used? Explain your answer.
4 a) What questions must you ask about the sources in this book before you rely on them?
   b) Why is this going to make studying the war difficult?

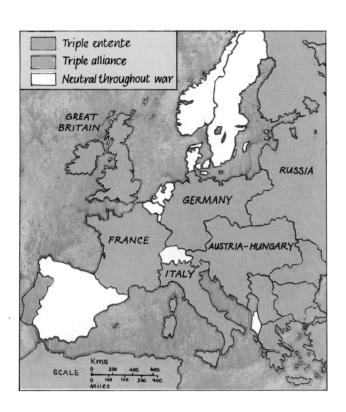

Key:
- Triple entente
- Triple alliance
- Neutral throughout war

GREAT BRITAIN, RUSSIA, GERMANY, FRANCE, AUSTRIA-HUNGARY, ITALY

SCALE
Kms 0 200 400 600
Miles 0 100 200 300 400

A The alliances of Europe in 1914.

Europe was tense in the years before 1914. All the major European powers were involved in one of two great alliances. These had grown up because the members felt they would be safer, knowing they had allies. But these alliances included military plans, just in case there was a war. So there was a risk that these agreements might actually drag countries into a war. Every European country had its war plans ready, just in case.

Most of Europe was ruled by great empires – British, German, Austro-Hungarian and Russian. Of them all, Britain felt most secure. Almost one quarter of the world was part of the British Empire. The British navy patrolled the oceans of the world, keeping one eye on the empire – and the other on what the Triple Alliance was up to. It aimed to be bigger than both the German and Austro-Hungarian navies put together.

And that gives us one clue why the war happened. Britain and Germany had become great rivals. Kaiser William II of Germany also wanted an empire; he, too, had been building up his navy;

by 1914, his industry was producing more iron, steel and coal than Britain was. Germany had become powerful.

The event which led to war happened in an unlikely place. On 28 June, Archduke Franz Ferdinand and his wife visited the small town of Sarajevo. It was in the south of the Austro-Hungarian empire. The Archduke was heir to the Austrian throne.

Travelling through the town, the Archduke was shot dead by a Serbian student called Gavrilo Princip. It made headline news the next day, then most Britons forgot about it. Sarajevo was a long way away; few people had ever heard of it.

But the Austrians did not forget. Austria sent Serbia an ultimatum : agree to our demands or we will declare war. Serbia agreed to most of these demands but not all. That did not satisfy the Austrian government. On 28 July, Austria declared war.

THE WORLD IS MINE

THE DREAM

B The Kaiser wanted to build up a great empire, like the British. This postcard of 1915 shows what the British thought of this.

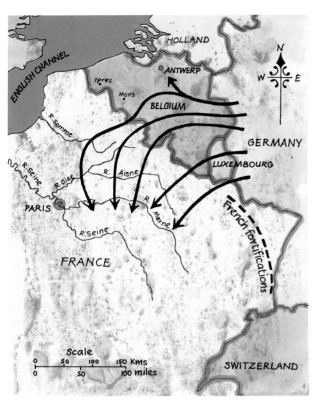

E In 1906, Britain launched a new class of battleship – HMS Dreadnought. It was quicker and better-armed than earlier ships. In 1914, Britain had 29 dreadnought battleships; Germany had 17.

C The Schlieffen Plan: Germany's plan to attack France (1914).

The German war plan had been drawn up in 1905 by Count Alfred von Schlieffen, who was then War Minister. He wanted to avoid having to fight France and Russia at the same time. So he planned to defeat France quickly and then send his troops to fight Russia.

But there was a problem. There were strong French defences on the border with Germany. Von Schlieffen solved this problem by planning an invasion of France through Belgium. Here, the French defences were weaker. But this only created a new problem. Belgium was neutral and Britain had promised in 1839 to support Belgium if the country were attacked.

D The countdown to war. How the alliances dragged the great powers into war.

28 July:	Austria-Hungary declared war on Serbia.
29 July:	Russia mobilised her army to support Serbia.
1 August:	Germany declared war on Russia.
3 August:	Germany declared war on France.
4 August:	Germany invaded Belgium. Britain declared war on Germany.
6 August:	Austria-Hungary declared war on Russia.
13 August:	France and Britain declared war on Austria-Hungary.

Historians study the causes of events. They try to discover different kinds of causes, such as long-term and short-term ones. They also try to decide which causes were most important. These two pages do not cover all the causes of war but they include both long-term and short-term causes.

1 a) Look at source A. Why would Germany feel threatened by this arrangement?
b) Why would Germany feel threatened by source E?
c) Why would Britain feel threatened by source C?
d) What threat to Britain does source B suggest?

2 a) Write down all the causes of the war which you can find.
b) Which of these was a short-term cause? Explain how you decided.
c) Which do you think were the most important causes? Give detailed reasons.

3 a) What were the links between Belgium, the Schlieffen Plan and Britain?
b) What is the link between sources B and E?
c) Why did Britain fight in the war? Explain your answer in detail.

| 1914 | 1915 | 1916 | 1917 | 1918 | 1919 |

A An early recruitment poster. The first ones appeared on 6 August, 1914.

People throughout Europe were delighted when war was announced. It was the most popular war in history. Everyone thought that their own country would win. In London, people bought Union Jacks and marched to Buckingham Palace; a smaller crowd smashed windows at the German Embassy.

But Britain had a problem. Both Germany and France forced their young men to join the forces. As a result, the German army had over two million men; even the French had a million and a quarter.

By comparison, the British army was tiny. In August, the British Expeditionary Force (BEF) set off for Belgium: it numbered just over 100,000 soldiers. Britain needed more men – fast.

The government did not want to force men to join the army so Lord Kitchener, the War Minister, had to ask for volunteers. The response was amazing: in August alone, 500,000 men enlisted. There were so many recruits that some had to train with umbrellas and broom handles: there weren't enough rifles to go round. There was even a national appeal for secondhand clothes: there weren't enough uniforms, either.

In August 1914, few people thought the war would last much beyond a few months. Most men probably volunteered because they thought it was their duty: Britain had to defend poor Belgium and teach the Germans a lesson. War also seemed to promise adventure: for many, it was a chance to escape from poverty and unemployment.

Many went to fight in what were called 'Pals' Battalions'. Each of these battalions was made up of men who already knew each other. For instance, ex-pupils of Wintringham Secondary School in Grimsby formed the 'Grimsby Chums'.

The men who joined the 'Pals' Battalions' usually trained together and went off to France together. Old school-friends marched side by side into the attack. Many of the 'Pals' died together.

Although men volunteered, they were under a lot of pressure. In London, women handed out white feathers to any man not in uniform. Music-hall stars also encouraged their audiences to enlist. And, of course, there were plenty of posters persuading men to go and fight.

B Perhaps the most famous poster of the war. Lord Kitchener tells men to enlist. He did not believe the war would be over quickly.

Daddy, what did YOU do in the Great War?

C Another recruiting poster.

The Schlieffen Plan did not go according to plan. In late August, the BEF fought the Germans at the Battle of Mons. The BEF was forced to retreat but not before it had delayed the German advance. The British people were not told of the retreat.

In September, the French defeated the German army at the Battle of the Marne; the Germans retreated – but the German people were not told. However, the German commander told the Kaiser, 'We have lost the war.'

The Germans turned north to get to the English Channel but were stopped at the Battle of Ypres. Any hope of a quick war was now over. As winter closed in, each side dug trenches to protect its position. Already, people were calling it 'the Great War'.

Why join up?

D The Accrington Pals were just one battalion created by Lord Kitchener. Peter Crookston described conditions in Lancashire at the time (1988).

East Lancashire was suffering from a recession in the cotton industry; 7000 workers were unemployed or working only part-time; 600 families were on relief and 700 children were fed by the council each lunchtime at the town hall. Army pay and allowances [amounted] to £1.05 a week, at a time when a skilled man could earn only £1.25. Poverty became the battalion's best recruiting sergeant.

E Wilf Hunt gave his reasons for joining up (TV interview, 1980s).

When the war broke out we was at Scarborough and we saw these reservists on their way up to the barracks. Seeing the war was going to be over in about six months, it was a good chance to have a decent holiday. We all went down to Leeds and joined the cavalry.

F Leslie Walkinton had his 17th birthday on 29 July 1914. He described his feelings in his autobiography, *Twice in a Lifetime* (1980).

[I had] a fear that I wouldn't be able to get into the Army because of my youth. I was painfully conscious of the fact that I didn't look a day older than my 17 years. It would be too terrible if the War did happen and I couldn't enlist!

I sought out a friend and we talked things over. Since there was a war, we must be in it. I think that we thought the limit of our activities would be guarding a railway bridge or something of that sort. Had we known that we would be in France within twelve weeks we would have been keener than ever, though perhaps slightly nervous.

G Captain Greig wrote to his parents in early 1915.

I feel that I shall come through this war, but one never knows. Whatever happens it is better that I should be doing my share than to be amongst the crowd who are doing nothing.

1 a) Look carefully at source C. What are the two children doing?
b) What do you think the man is supposed to be thinking? Explain how you decided.
2 a) Be careful. Who is telling men to enlist in each of the posters?
b) What feeling does each poster try to stir up? Explain how you decided.
c) Which poster would have had most effect on you? Give reasons for your choice.

3 a) Write down all the reasons you can find why men enlisted.
b) How does source D support the text on page 8?
c) Which of the sources (if any) do you think might not be reliable? Explain how you decided.
4 Sources A, B and C are all propaganda. How, then, can they be useful to historians? Please answer in detail.

| 1914 | 1915 | 1916 | 1917 | 1918 | 1919 |

A A rare photograph of an attack in progress. It was taken by a soldier in the Liverpool Scottish Battalion in 1915.

By the end of 1914, the trenches stretched from the Channel coast to Switzerland – over 370 miles (600km) of them. In the next four years, they rarely moved more than 10 miles (16km) either west or east.

This line of trenches was the Western Front. In time, more lines of trenches were dug behind them; they were linked up by communication trenches. For every 1½km of front, there were eventually 30 miles (48km) of trenches. On the Eastern Front, Germans and Russians also dug trenches facing each other. In front of the trenches was stretched a barrier of barbed wire, up to 15 metres thick.

In between was No Man's Land – the area which was being fought over. The two trench lines could be as much as 800 metres apart; in a few places, the enemy was just 20 metres away. Every night, patrols were sent out into the area to find out what the enemy was doing.

The aim was to capture the enemy's trenches but this was difficult because they were so well-defended. The ordinary soldier carried a bayonet and a rifle which fired up to 25 shots per minute. These were no match for machine-guns which fired 600 rounds a minute.

The generals believed that they could win by sending huge numbers of men across No Man's Land to capture enemy trenches. For days beforehand, artillery would bombard the enemy night and day. The idea was that the shells would destroy enemy wire and trenches, making attack easier. But, in wet weather, they turned No Man's Land into a sea of mud, making it harder to get across.

Even in dry weather, an attack would cause huge casualties. The barrage warned the enemy that an attack was coming. When it stopped, the attack began. An officer blew a whistle and the men went 'over the top' of the trench and ran towards the enemy.

All too often, the enemy's machine-guns just mowed them down. The generals were trying to fight an offensive war – but the best weapons were defensive.

In one way, the Great War was unique. It was the only major war ever fought without voice control. In other words, once an attack started, the generals had no control over their troops. So the men were given their instructions and told to stick to them. On the day, the generals were too far away to know whether they were appropriate or not.

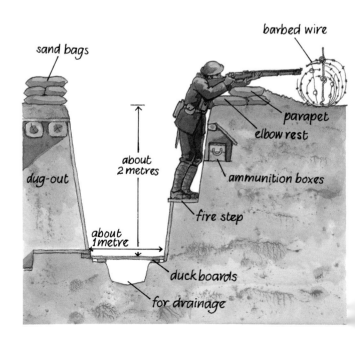

B This was what a trench looked like in theory. It was described to soldiers during training.

For over 70 years, historians have argued about the tactics used in the war. Some have believed that they were suicidal and foolish; others claim that the commanders had the right idea and that there was no real alternative. Historians often offer different interpretations like this. The reader must judge which interpretation is better.

1 a) Describe what you can see in source A.
   b) Describe what you can see in source C.
   c) Which source is more useful for understanding what an attack was like? Give reasons for your choice.
   d) 'Photographs are more reliable than paintings.' Do you agree? Give reasons.
   e) How does the trench in source C differ from source B?
   f) How is source B useful for our understanding of the war?

2 a) Read sources E and F. What are their criticisms of the generals?
   b) Does source D support the generals or not? Explain your answer.
   c) Of all the sources, which is most useful for understanding why so many men were killed? Give detailed reasons.

C This painting shows Canadian troops being attacked by the Germans in 1915.

D Charles Messenger: *Trench Fighting* (1972).
It has been fashionable to criticise the generals on the Western Front. But it must be remembered that they were all faced with an entirely new situation, of which they had no previous experience. The task of the general in war is to win victories and these are not won by sitting still. Sooner or later one must attack and they did their best to do this with the tools available.

E An American historian, Richard Watt, gave his view in *Dare Call It Treason* (1963).
The generals are to be blamed not so much because they failed to open up the trench war as because they *went on trying to do it*, wasting thousands of lives with each attempt, long after it should have been [clear] that they could not succeed with the old methods.

F *The American Heritage History of World War One* (1964).
Too often, the front line rested on a marshy flat, with strong slopes [behind it]. General Smith-Dorrien was relieved of command of the Second Army, simply because he doubted that offensive operations were justified. [He] wanted to yield some ground at Ypres so that his troops would be less exposed.

LIFE IN THE TRENCHES

Daily routine did not change much, unless there was an attack. Half an hour before sunrise there was an order to 'stand-to'. Everyone stood on the firestep, in case there was an attack. Afterwards, sentries were posted and the men ate breakfast.

The meal was followed by inspection. Then, the day was taken up with routine jobs, mostly to do with keeping the trenches in good repair. This continued until another 'stand-to' at dusk. Finally, the rations arrived and the day was over.

In some parts of the line, the two sides had an unspoken agreement to 'live and let live'. For instance, the sides might not shell each other's latrines or open fire during breakfast.

The most famous example was on Christmas Day, 1914. Ceasefires were agreed over two-thirds of the British line. The two enemies met up in No Man's Land and exchanged Christmas presents of food and cigars. Some even played football.

In some areas, the friendship went on for days (or even weeks) afterwards. Days later, some Germans even sent an apology when a British soldier was killed. But the generals ordered that it should never happen again. In later years, 25 December was a day like any other.

Food did not vary much, either. It was usually bread and biscuits, with tins of 'bully beef' to heat up; this was a bit like modern corned beef. The big army biscuits were so hard that troops hit them with bayonets to break them.

The trenches themselves were not just dangerous places to be; they were dirty and unhealthy. Clothes were infested with lice, which left red blotches on the body. When off-duty, men killed them with lighted candles: they went 'pop'.

Many soldiers feared rats even more than shell fire. They were everywhere. They fed off the food scraps and dead bodies: eyes and livers were their favourite parts. Sometimes, they attacked those who were dying or just sleeping. Soldiers reckoned that rats could sense when shellfire was about to start. When it did begin, the animals screamed with terror.

Some men could not cope. Some developed 'trench fever' and could not stop themselves shaking; today, we would call this 'shell shock'. A few tried to run away: their punishment was execution by a firing squad. Others gave themselves a 'blighty wound' in order to get sent back to blighty (home). Read the sources and you may see why.

A The trenches often flooded, as in this 1915 painting. Standing too long in cold water could cause an illness called 'trench foot'.

B Food for the soldiers: a photograph of a French abattoir.

C Stuart Cloete: *Victorian Son: An Autobiography* (1972).

Burial was impossible. There were hundreds, thousands [of bodies a day], not merely ours but Germans as well. And where we fought several times over the same ground, bodies became [part of] the material of the trenches themselves. In one place we had to dig through corpses of Frenchmen who had been buried in 1915. These bodies were [rotten]. I once fell and put my hand right through the belly of a man. It was days before I got the smell out of my nails.

D Robert Graves: *Goodbye to all That* (1957).

The familiar trench smell still haunts my nostrils: [mixed] of mud, latrine buckets, chloride of lime, unburied or half-buried corpses, rotting sandbags, stale human sweat. Sometimes it was sweetened by cigarette smoke and the scent of bacon frying over wood fires.

E A Stuart Dolden: *Cannon Fodder* (1980).

The area was infested with [rats]. They grew fat on the food that they [stole] from us, and anything they could pick up in or around the trenches; they were bloated and loathsome to look on. One night a rat ran across my face. Unfortunately my mouth happened to be open and the hind legs of the filthy little beast went right in.

F Dead bodies were everywhere. Shellfire uncovered this dead French soldier in a British trench.

G Arthur Borton wrote home to his wife in October 1916:

We come out for a rest the day after tomorrow, and I shall be glad of it. I HAVEN'T HAD MY BOOTS OR CLOTHING OFF FOR FIVE DAYS AND NIGHTS and haven't had a bath for a fortnight.

H George Coppard: *With a Machine-gun to Cambrai* (1980).

The fire was going nicely and the bacon was sizzling. I was sitting on the firestep. Just as I was about to tuck in, Bill crashed to the ground. We carried Bill to the first aid post after putting some bandages round his head to hide the mess. He died later that morning.

When we got back to the front line we were ravenous with hunger. My bacon and bread was on the fire step, but covered with dirt and pieces of Bill's brain. I inspected the front of my tunic and trousers and there were more bits there; my boots were sticky with blood.

I William Pressey: *All For a Shilling a Day* (1973).

If anyone had [asked] they would have been told that every soldier got half a loaf of bread a day. We never got this once. Many, many times we had one slice only for breakfast and for tea hard biscuits. They were so hard that I've held one in my hand and hit the sharp corner on a brick wall and only hurt my hand.

1 Explain the meaning of these words: stand-to; bully beef; No Man's Land; trench fever; blighty wound.

2 a) Look at sources A and B. How do they help you to understand trench life?

b) Which one gives you the better idea of trench life? Give reasons for your choice.

c) Does it make any difference that one is a painting and one is a photograph? Explain your answer.

3 a) Each written source refers to one aspect of trench life. Write down what each one is.

b) Describe trench life, using only the written sources.

c) What other aspects of trench life would you want evidence of? Explain why they would be important.

4 a) Some of the sources were written long after the war. Does that mean that they are unreliable? Explain your answer.

b) 'The letter is the best source to use because it was written at the time.' Explain whether you agree with this statement.

ASSESSING THE SOURCES

A British gunner delivering the post in 1916. Pictures like this were later sold to the public.

Life in the trenches was not all fighting. In fact, about 10 per cent was action and 90 per cent was boredom. But the artillery did not stop. About 30 shells a minute would be fired during a major bombardment. The sound could be heard in England as far north as Cambridge. In the trenches, the noise must have been incredible.

As the war spread, there was fighting in many parts of the world – in Africa and Austria, Greece and Palestine. But the heaviest fighting took place in the trenches of the Western Front. When people talk of the Great War, they think of trenches.

There is plenty of evidence about trench life so we ought to be able to find out what it was like at the front. But sources are not always reliable. For instance, official photographers were rarely present when it was dangerous. So there are few genuine photographs of attacks. In any case, official pictures were often shot to use as propaganda.

Paintings offer a more detailed view of battles, as you have seen. But they rarely give an accurate picture of what happened. This was especially true of attacks: painters generally showed the opposing armies closer together than they really were.

There are thousands of written accounts but, for each one, we must ask how true and accurate it is. Lloyd George, the British Prime Minister, believed the public would want to stop the war – if they knew how bad it was. 'But they can't know,' he said. 'The censorship wouldn't pass the truth.'

B Even modern books often ignore certain aspects of trench life. John Laffin wrote about latrines in *The Western Front Illustrated* (1991). Practically nothing has been written about latrines, but they were an important part of a trench system. Trench latrines were supposed to be pits dug 4ft to 5ft deep, in a special sap . When filled to within a foot of the top they were filled in and a new one dug. The actual practice varied greatly.

At various times metal buckets were used, again in a special sap. When filled, the contents of the buckets were to be buried between the front and support trenches but, often as not, soldiers simply threw it as far as possible.

C This advertisement was made in 1915.

D Picture postcards rarely showed dead soldiers. This Dutch one is an exception. Dead men's boots were taken by the living.

E French troops in action, early in the war. Their blue uniforms were easy to spot and were later replaced by khaki .

F Another photograph of French troops in the war.

G On 4 July 1916, Arthur Borton wrote home to his father. This is part of the letter.

My dear Daddie,

I haven't had much time to write as have been pretty busy. We have been UP IN THE LINE now for 3 days. There has been a lot of SCRAPPING all around us. I wonder if you've been able to hear the row we've been making at [home]? We have remained so far in a kind of BACKWATER but don't suppose it will last.

Am in a very comfortable DUG-OUT with heaps of Head cover. But the mud is awful. Have had two days of rain which has flooded everything. And the RATS ARE A CAUTION. I didn't believe there were so many in the country. Black as well as brown. In fact I'm fed up with the war. French life is not what it is cracked up to be.

H That same day, Arthur Borton also wrote to his wife:

. . . Am very comfortable in my present quarters. We are living in a HOLE IN THE GROUND formerly occupied by a FRENCH GENERAL, and IT'S SOME HOLE! 8 stairs down, 3 Large Rooms – Glass windows, wooden flooring, tables, chairs and bedsteads etc.

Many sources are unreliable in some way. As you study each source on these pages, ask yourself whether there is any reason to have doubts about it. But remember that even the most unreliable sources are often useful. For instance, a propaganda photograph shows us what the government wanted people to think.

1 a) Look at each picture in turn. Write down why you think each one was made. (If necessary, make a guess.)
b) Write down whether you think each picture is reliable or not. In each case, explain how you decided.
c) Think about those that you have chosen as not reliable. What can a historian learn from each of them? (Different answers, please.)
d) What questions do you need to ask about sources before you rely on them? You should think of at least three.

2 If you could use only one of these pictures to illustrate trench life, which would you use? Give reasons.

3 a) Read sources G and H. What different ideas of trench life do they give?
b) Suggest at least one reason why they disagree.
c) Which one do you think gives the more reliable idea of the man's circumstances? Give reasons.

STALEMATE

Throughout the winter of 1914-15, soldiers dug their trenches. It had become clear that this was not going to be a quick war. Once the troops were dug in, major attacks could not be organised quickly or easily. Fresh soldiers had to be brought up and the big guns wheeled into position. Telephone lines had to be laid and food supplies organised.

The generals already knew how costly battles could be. The first Battle of Ypres in October-November 1914 killed 130,000 Germans and 58,000 British. Lord Kitchener was appalled. 'This isn't war!' he exclaimed.

In fact, no one had prepared for this kind of war. The war plans had assumed it would be a war of movement. Behind the lines, the cavalry waited to make heroic charges which rarely happened. Instead, it had become a war of attrition . In other words, each side tried to wear down the enemy.

A   This painting shows a landing in Gallipoli, 1915. It was painted on the spot, using dye from cigarette packets.

Some Allied politicians and generals thought the answer was to attack elsewhere. In October 1914, Turkey had joined the war on the German side. Some politicians believed that attacking Turkey might break the deadlock. It might force the Germans to take troops from the Western Front. And *that* might give the Allies the chance of a breakthrough.

The Allies made two attempts to defeat the Turks. A naval attack in early 1915 failed. An army attack on the Gallipoli pensinsula in April did no better. Turkish machine-guns mowed down Allied troops as they came ashore. (Many of these guns had been manufactured in Britain.) So the Allies went on the defensive: they dug trenches.

Attacking Turkey did not end the war quickly. Indeed, it cost the lives of men who could have been used on the Western Front. Now, all eyes turned back to the west. The new British commander-in-chief was Sir Douglas Haig. He had been convinced all along that the war could only be won in the west. The year 1916 gave him a chance to find out if he was right.

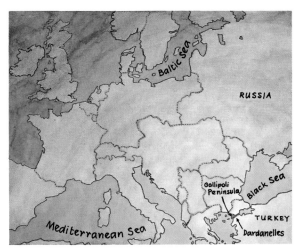

B Where the Allies attacked Turkey in 1915.

Ammunition problems

C Lt-Colonel Drake-Brockman described the shortage of shells in early 1915.

In any attack, [the Germans] used plenty of ammunition. We were far behind them in these early days of the war, and could not effectively reply. If one telephoned the gunner officer for a little ammunition to be [used], the reply generally was: 'Sorry, but I have used my allowance!' This was, at that time, eighteen rounds daily per battery .

D From the diary of Sir John French, commander of the BEF until December 1915.

[Kitchener] is firmly convinced that we *waste* ammunition here. I told him quite plainly that neither he nor his advisers had any [idea] of what modern war was really like. The enemy's trenches must be broken down, his wire torn up, and the machine-gun resistance reduced by artillery fire and an unlimited amount of ammunition.

E The ammunition shortage: a British cartoon (1915).

F Lloyd George became British Minister of Munitions in July. This is what he said in April.

The Secretary of State informs me that the production of high explosives [is of a level] which relieves us of all anxiety. [It] enables us, in addition, to supply our Allies.

G Anthony Bruce: *An Illustrated Companion to The First World War* (1989).

Massive artillery attacks achieved very little. In the first part of the war, British artillery shells were in short supply and were often of very poor quality. They churned up the ground and, combined with rain, affected the progress of advancing forces.

In July 1915, [Lloyd George] was appointed to the new post of Minister of Munitions. He planned a massive expansion in the production of ammunition and weapons. Manufacturers were [coaxed] or bribed into producing more.

1 a) In Source E, who is asking for help?
   b) Who are the people who are too busy to help?
   c) What was the cartoonist's attitude? Explain how you decided.
2 a) Which of the written sources suggest that a shortage of ammunition was a problem?
   b) Think about source C. Why was an ammunition shortage a problem?
   c) Why was more ammunition needed according to D?
   d) How does source G suggest that more ammunition would not have helped?
   e) How do sources F and G disagree?
   f) Does that mean that the Secretary of State was lying? Explain your answer carefully.

It has been said that the Great War was a war in which men fought machines – and the machines won. It was certainly a war in which heavy artillery did most of the damage.

The Germans appreciated the importance of machinery better than France or Britain in 1914. They had far more machine-guns and they also had a surprise artillery weapon. It was a massive gun which fired shells which were as tall as a soldier. The men nicknamed it 'Big Bertha'. Its huge shells easily destroyed Belgian forts in 1914.

All the armies used camouflage. A few cavalry regiments began the war dressed in bright red, green or blue. But fairly quickly both officers and men switched to khaki. It blended well with the mud of the trenches. The Scots Greys even dyed their horses so that they would not be seen so easily.

A A camouflaged cannon from later in the war.

But the Great War is remembered as being a war of new weapons. One of them was gas. The French used tear gas as early as August 1914. In October, the Germans replied with shells treated with chemicals which acted as an irritant. They weren't any good: the Allies did not know they had been used until the war was over! But far worse was to come.

B One of these French soldiers is prepared for a gas attack.

On 22 April 1915, the Germans set off over 168 tons of chlorine gas. If you inhale chlorine for more than a couple of minutes, it kills you. That day, 5,000 Allied troops were killed and another 10,000 injured.

A new method of attack led to new methods of defence. The early advice was to soak a handkerchief in urine or bicarbonate of soda; gas masks soon followed; in 1916, the box respirator appeared. Dogs and horses were also given gas masks. About 7 per cent of human gas casualties died; most went back into action.

Meanwhile, the Germans had begun using phosgene, another choking gas, but more deadly than chlorine. But each had one key disadvantage: the wind could shift and blow it backwards – straight onto your own troops. One solution was to put the gas into shells and fire them at the enemy.

Gas

C Sir Arthur Conan Doyle gave his opinion of gas in *The British Campaigns in Europe 1914-1918* (1928).

The Germans [won] ground by the arts of the murderer. A great army became in a single day an object of horror and contempt.

D Anthony Bruce: *An Illustrated Companion to the First World War* (1989).

Germany's reputation was damaged by her first use of gas, although 'both experience and statistics proved it to be the least [cruel] of modern weapons'.

E Anthony R Hossack: *The First Gas Attack* (1930). He was an eye-witness.

Along either side of [the road] lay more than eight hundred men, with foam upon their lips, clutching at their mouths, their faces inhuman in colour; a month later, when I reached the great hospital at Le Tréport, a few of them still lived but none of them could speak.

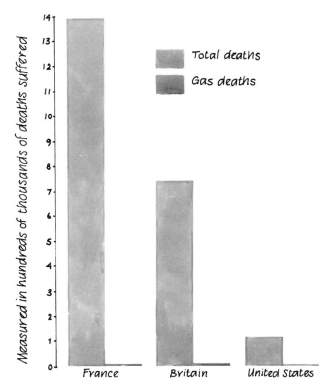

F Totals of troops killed in the war, compared with deaths by gassing. All war casualty figures are only roughly correct.

G J M Bourne: *Britain and the Great War* (1989).

As late as the 1960s, Coroners' reports regularly drew attention to war service, especially gassing, as a contributory cause of death.

H German soldiers wearing protective gear.

Secondary sources often offer different interpretations of what happened. We need to compare these with other evidence to decide which interpretation seems most likely to be true.

1 a) Look at source A. How is this gun camouflaged?
b) Look at sources B and H. Which picture is from later in the war? Explain how you decided.

2 a) Read sources C and D carefully. How do they disagree about the use of gas?
b) What opinions does the writer of source C give? Quote from the source in your answer.
c) Does source E support source C or D? Give a reason.
d) Which source does source F support? Give reasons.
e) How does source G add to your understanding of source F?
f) Do you agree with source C or source D? Answer carefully.

By early 1916, each side was waging a war of attrition. Put simply, the aim was to kill more of the enemy than they killed of you. A huge German attack on Verdun weakened the French army. Meanwhile, Sir Douglas Haig planned a major British attack on the Germans.

The place chosen was the River Somme. It was an odd choice. The land sloped upwards towards the German lines so the German trenches were on high ground. In addition, the land was chalky. So the Germans had easily dug very deep front-line trenches.

The Germans knew the attack was coming. For seven days, British artillery pounded the German front line. Mostly, the shells fell on empty trenches. The bulk of the German soldiers were in dug-outs up to 12 metres below ground level.

The attack began at 7.30am on 1 July 1916. It was a sunny summer morning. The plan was that over 500,000 men would cross No Man's Land and capture the enemy line. When they had broken through, the cavalry would ride straight through the gap.

A The *News of the World* printed this headline news on 2 July. In fact, it just repeats the official   communiqué .

BRITISH ADVANCE.

16 MILES OF GERMAN FRONT TRENCHES STORMED.

"THE DAY GOES WELL" FOR OUR HEROIC TROOPS.

Special Telegrams to the "News of the World."

British Headquarters, July 1.—Attack launched north of River Somme this morning at 7.30 a.m., in conjunction with French.

British troops have broken into German forward system of defences on front of 16 miles.

Fighting is continuing.

French attack on our immediate right proceeding equally satisfactorily.

On remainder of British front raiding parties again succeeded in penetrating enemy's defences at many points, inflicting loss on enemy and taking some prisoners.

FRENCH OFFICIAL.

B This British photograph was issued as a postcard. Its caption read: *'The Glorious First of July, 1916' – our first prisoners.*

C Entries in Sir Douglas Haig's diary.
30 June 1916
The men are in splendid spirits. Several have said that they have never been so informed of the nature of the operations before them. The wire has never been so well cut, nor the artillery preparation so thorough.
1 July 1916 (8.00am)
Reports [are] most satisfactory. Our troops had everywhere crossed the enemy's front trenches.

D Frank Lindley of the Barnsley Pals explained the orders in a TV programme (1980s).
We were told to walk over. Walk. Which, in itself, was stupid. And you had to go over in a line, walking. That was the stupid idea. But, still, we had to do what we were told.

E Reverend John Walker was at the Somme as a chaplain. This is his diary entry on 1 July.
7.30, the crazy hour had begun. Every gun we owned fired as hard as ever it could for more than an hour. We got back for a late breakfast and soon the wounded came in. Then, all day long cars of dying and wounded, but all cheerful for they told us of a day of glorious successes.

F George Coppard fought on the Somme. This is what he saw on the morning of 2 July. (From *With a Machine Gun to Cambrai*, 1980.)

It was clear that there were no gaps in the wire at the time of the attack. The Germans must have been reinforcing their wire for months. It was so dense that daylight could barely be seen through it. How did planners imagine that Tommies would get through the German wire? Any Tommy could have told them that shell fire lifts wire up and drops it down, often in a worse tangle than before.

G George Morgan was a member of the Bradford Pals Battalion. Sixty years later, he recalled 1 July.

We formed into one line and walked slowly forward. We had only gone a few yards when my mate, Billy Booth, was hit. Then the man on my left fell against me. Lines of men were just disappearing. The Germans' machine guns fired at us like it was target practice.

The wire was 60 yards away but only a few made it as far as that. They became fastened on the barbs and the machine guns tore their bodies to shreds. It was all over in ten minutes.

It was a slaughter. The commanders, Haig and Rawlinson, didn't care about us. I don't think they bothered about human life.

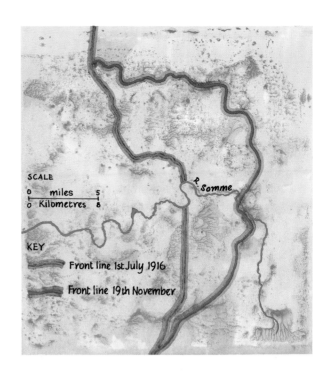

I Map of the battle area, showing how much land was gained.

J Approximate casualty figures for the battle (1 July–19 November).

> British Empire – 419,000
> French – 194,451
> Germans – 650,000

British losses on 1 July: 58,000 casualties, including 21,000 dead. This was the greatest loss ever suffered by the British army on one day. It was also the greatest loss of any army in the Great War.

Please give reasons for all your answers.

  1   a) Why did Haig (source C) think the attack would succeed?

b) Why were the men (source D) told to walk over?

c) Which sources suggest that the first day was a success?

d) Look at your answers to (c). Explain why each of these sources is unreliable.

e) How are these unreliable sources useful to a historian?

  2   a) Does source I show that the battle was a success or not?

b) Does source H show that the battle was a success or not?

  3   a) Which sources are most useful for understanding what happened on 1 July?

b) Which source is most useful for understanding why the attack went wrong?

H A painting of wounded troops arriving back in London in July 1916.

A A poem by A A Milne.

> Same old trenches, same old view,
> Same old rats as blooming tame,
> Same old dugouts, nothing new,
> Same old smell, the very same,
> Same old bodies out in front,
> Same old strafe from two till four,
> Same old scratching, same old hunt,
> Same old bloody war.

The troops had set off in August 1914, believing the war would be over by Christmas. By Christmas 1916, the fighting was still going on. Few people even thought an end was in sight.

Yet, on the Western Front, the armies battled it out over the same stretch of land, turning it into a wasteland. Many soldiers said it was not possible to describe the sight of a battlefield. This was one of them, photographed in 1917.

The Battle of the Somme had a great effect on the troops. Many now doubted the ability of their leaders. They felt betrayed. As a result, they lost some of their enthusiasm for the war. Back at home, a film called *Battle of the Somme* was shown in British cinemas in August 1916. It included film of an attack, shown in source C.

C

For the first time, people in Britain could *see* what the war was like. *The Times* said that people in future need only look at the film to see what trench conditions were like. But was this true?

Modern historians think that some of the film was taken in training trenches, away from the front line. In any case, the film never shows the enemy nor any real action. Above all, the film was silent. There was no sound of shells exploding or machine-guns firing.

However, civilians also learned about the war through letters sent home. They already knew that the men's attitudes were changing. This was bound to have an effect on those at home who might think of joining up.

D The real thing. The moment of death for a French soldier (arrowed) attacking a German trench in 1917.

ARE YOU A VICTIM TO
OPTIMISM?
—o—o—o—o—
YOU DON'T KNOW?
—o—o—o—o—
THEN ASK YOURSELF THE FOLLOWING QUESTIONS.
—o—o—o—o—

1.—DO YOU SUFFER FROM CHEERFULNESS?
2.—DO YOU WAKE UP IN A MORNING FEELING THAT ALL IS GOING WELL FOR THE ALLIES?
3.—DO YOU SOMETIMES THINK THAT THE WAR WILL END WITHIN THE NEXT TWELVE MONTHS?
4.—DO YOU BELIEVE GOOD NEWS IN PREFERENCE TO BAD?
5.—DO YOU CONSIDER OUR LEADERS ARE COMPETENT TO CONDUCT THE WAR TO A SUCCESSFUL ISSUE?

IF YOUR ANSWER IS "YES" TO ANYONE OF THESE QUESTIONS THEN YOU ARE IN THE CLUTCHES OF THAT DREAD DISEASE.

WE CAN CURE YOU.

TWO DAYS SPENT AT OUR ESTABLISHMENT WILL EFFECTUALLY ERADICATE ALL TRACES OF IT FROM YOUR SYSTEM.
DO NOT HESITATE—APPLY FOR TERMS AT ONCE TO:—

Messrs. Walthorpe, Foxley, Nelmes and Co.

TELEPHONE 72, "GRUMBLESTONES."   TELEGRAMS: "GROUSE."

E This mock advert appeared in *The Somme Times*, a trench newspaper published on 31 July 1916.

F Lieutenant Edward Chapman went to France during the Battle of the Somme. He fought for ten months before he was badly wounded in 1917. These extracts are from letters home.

July 1916
I am enjoying life hugely. I love the army – and it is a great game. I haven't seen war yet really, but I know I shall hate it. But army life is grand, and I wouldn't be a civilian just yet for anything.

August 1916
I hate all this business from the bottom of my soul. It has turned a beautiful country into a desolate waste. All this area is one vast cemetery. It has robbed thousands and thousands of men of life. I feel that all I want to do is to be able to live quietly, and tend a garden, and study a bit.

September 1916
Don't swallow all that the papers say about the 'great push'. When you read of German battalions being [destroyed], don't forget that English battalions get wiped out too.

September 1916 (out of the front line)
This is a jolly life, but it is not war. The three weeks in the Somme area pretty well knocked me out but I feel fit for anything again now – even the Somme if necessary.

1 a) Look carefully at source B. What signs of war are there?
b) Suppose you had been fighting at the place shown in source B. Write a description of it to send home.
c) Was this easy or difficult? Give reasons.
2 a) Had the writer of source A changed his view of the war? Explain your answer.
b) Read source F. How do the writer's attitudes change? Answer in detail.
c) Why did attitudes change? You should find at least three different reasons.

| 1914 | 1915 | 1916 | 1917 | 1918 | 1919 |

We'll Shed the Old
And Don the New
For we're Going to See
This Business through.

A In May 1918, the age limit was raised to 50. This postcard reminded people.

During 1916, there had been one big change. By January, about 550,000 British soldiers were already dead or wounded. (After March, the government did not release official casualty figures.) The country needed 5,000 volunteers every week to fill the gap.

Germany already used conscription: in other words, men were forced to join up. In January 1916, the British government followed suit. Every unmarried man aged between 18 and 41 had to enlist. In May, another Act of Parliament enlisted all married men in the same age group.

However, some men were allowed to stay in Britain. They included those who were not fit enough, as well as those who were doing essential jobs. This covered people like miners and engine drivers – people whose work was necessary to keep the country going.

Special tribunals were set up to listen to those who thought they had a right to stay at home. They also listened to the arguments of pacifists – people who thought it was wrong to fight and kill.

The tribunals were not very sympathetic to pacifists. Officially, they were called conscientious objectors or COs but they were usually known as 'conshies'. Other nicknames were even less pleasant: the newspapers called them 'slackers' and 'shirkers'.

Altogether, there were about 16,000 COs. Many of them took on jobs such as driving ambulances and helped in the war effort. But about 1,500 absolutely refused to have anything at all to do with the war. They were sent to prison, where they were not allowed to speak. At first, they were not allowed to write letters for eight weeks. This was later reduced to fortnightly intervals.

Seventy-one COs died in prison or as a result of their treatment during the war; another 31 had become mentally unstable. In 1918, COs were banned from voting for five years. On top of that, they were only released six months after the war ended. This made sure that ex-soldiers had the first pick of jobs.

B This cartoon appeared in a pacifist newspaper during the war.

WHEN·HANDED OVER·TO·THE· MILITARY·BY· CIVIL·AUTHORITY

ON·SEEING· THE·PRISON· WALL·····

WHEN·ADDRESSING·HIS· ·COURT-MARTIAL·

WHEN·BEING·EXAMINED ·BY·THE·PRISON·DOCTOR

IN·PRISON·CLOTHING

WHAT·A·C.O. WILL·FEEL· LIKE·WHEN HE·GETS· HIS·FINAL DISCHARGE

WHEN·HE·ARRIVES ON·THE·HOME···· OFFICE·SCHEME·····

C This pacifist postcard was printed in 1917.

D One CO told this story of meeting some soldiers who were under arrest.

Right at the beginning I learnt that the only people from whom I was to expect sympathy were the soldiers, and not the civilians.

When I was waiting in [the] guard-room, five men were bustled into the room, and the door was slammed on them.

One of [the soldiers] walked up to me.

'What are you in here for, mate?'

I thought it best to be as simple as possible, so I said:

'Well, you see I am a Quaker , and I refused to join the army, because I think that war is murder.'

The man took a step backwards. A terrible light came into his eyes. He raised his arm, which had a wound stripe on it. I thought that he was going to spring at me. The room was very silent.

'Murder?' he whispered. 'Murder? It's *bloody* murder.'

And then we were friends. We had only a little while together, because the men were soon marched away and I never saw them again. But as they went, they each came up to me, and shook me by the hand.

'Stick to it, matey! Stick!' they said, one after another.

E Percy Wall failed to enlist when he was sent his call-up papers. He was sent to a military camp. He described his time there.

The attitude of the soldiers towards us during the time we were at camp fell roughly in three divisions. A very small minority told us they would like to see us shot. [Others] wished to know exactly what we were standing for and some of them told us they would be COs next time. Another section seemed to think we wanted to get out of going to the trenches (as they admitted they did). These seemed unable to understand a matter of principle at all.

F The Commander of the Military Detention Barracks at Wandsworth explained his way of dealing with COs in a letter to the *Daily Express* (1916).

I had them placed in special rooms, nude, but with their full army kit on the floor for them to put on as soon as they [wished]. There were no blankets or substitutes for clothing left in the rooms which were quite bare. Several of the men held out naked for several hours but they gradually accepted the inevitable. Forty of the conscientious objectors who passed through my hands are now quite willing soldiers.

G Headline in a British newspaper, 1916.
NEW NAME FOR SLACKERS – CONSCIENTIOUS OBJECTORS

Most people supported the war and believed it was right to fight Germany. But, at any time, there are always some people who do not agree with the views of the majority. Conscientious objectors disagreed with the views of most British people in 1914-18.

1 a) What did most people feel about the war in 1914?
b) What did the CO in source D feel about the war?
c) Why did he feel differently?

2 a) Look at source B. How has the artist drawn the businessman and the soldier?
b) What does this tell you about what the artist felt about the war?

3 a) Look at source C. How does the CO feel in pictures 1, 2 and 3?
b) Why should he feel like this?
c) What point is the artist making in picture 7?

4 a) What was the attitude of the soldiers in sources D and E?
b) Why do you think soldiers were often more sympathetic than civilians?

The troops sang on their way to war; they sang on the march; they sang in the trenches; they sang on the way home. There was no shortage of popular songs but the men often went one better. They made up their own, often using popular tunes, or they changed the words. Some of them are on these two pages.

A When the German army failed to move quickly through Belgium at the start of the war soldiers sang:

Belgium put the kibosh on the Kaiser;
Europe took a stick and made him sore;
We shall shout with victory's joy,
Hold your hand out, naughty boy,
You must never play at soldiers any more.

B One of the most popular songs of 1914 was written by the Welsh composer Ivor Novello.

They were summoned from the hillside,
They were called in from the glen,
And the country found them ready,
At the stirring call for men.
Let no tears add to their hardship,
As the soldiers pass along,
And although your heart is breaking,
Make it sing this cheery song:

TILL THE BOYS COME HOME (2).
Keep the home-fires burning, while your hearts are yearning,
Though your lads are far away they dream of home;
There's a silver lining through the dark cloud shining:
Turn the dark cloud inside out, till the boys come home.

C This postcard gives the chorus to source B.

D Leslie Walkinton was on sick leave from the trenches when he heard Novello sing his song. (From *Twice in a Lifetime*, 1980.)

One of the performers was Ivor Novello, who later became well known. He sang a song which he had written himself called *Keep the Home Fires Burning*.

We thought it poor sentimental mush. I heard a tough-looking Tommy say very seriously to his pal: 'Don't laugh at 'im. It's what blokes like that thinks is doin' their bit.' When he left, Mr Novello gave each of us a packet of cigarettes for which we were very grateful.

"IT'S A LONG, LONG WAY FROM TIPPERARY."

IN ACTION—DRIVING BACK THE HUNS.
Molly wrote a neat reply to Irish Paddy O',
 Saying " Mike Maloney wants to marry me, and so
Leave the Strand and Piccadilly or you'll be to blame,
 For love has fairly drove me silly—hoping you're the same ! "
" It's a long way fo Tipperary, it's a long way to go;
It's a long way to Tipperary, to the sweetest girl I know!
Good-bye Piccadilly, farewell Leicester Square,
It's a long, long way to Tipperary, but my heart's right there ! "
By permission of B. Feldman & Co., 2 & 3 Arthur St., London, W.C.

E This pre-war song became so popular that even the Germans sang it.

F In 1917, one of the year's big successes was 'Good-Bye-Ee'.

Goodbye-ee, Goodbye-ee,
Wipe the tear, baby dear, from your eye-ee,
Tho' it's hard to part I know, I'll be tickled to death to go.
Don't cry-ee, don't sigh-ee, there's a silver lining in the sky-ee,
Bonsoir, old thing, cheerio, chin, chin,
Nap-poo, toodle-oo, Goodbye-ee.

TAKE ME BACK TO DEAR OLD BLIGHTY. (2).

Take me back to dear old Blighty, put me on the train —.
for London town,
Take me over there, drop me anywhere,
Birmingham, Leeds, or Manchester—well, I don't care !
I should love to see my best girl, cuddling up again we
soon shall be ;
Whoa ! Tiddley-iddley-ighty, hurry me home to Blighty—
Blighty is the place for me.

BAMFORTH COPYRIGHT.   WORDS BY PERMISSION OF THE STAR MUSIC PUBLISHING CO. LONDON

G This was the chorus of one of 1916's popular songs.

These were well-known songs. Some of the soldiers' songs are now long-forgotten. Here is a selection of those that have survived.

H This one summed up feelings about the war:
Why did we join the Army, boys?
Why did we join the Army?
Why did we come to France to fight?
We must have been bloody well barmy.

I This song became common from 1916 onwards. Various lyrics were used.
When this bloody war is over
Oh, how happy I will be!
When I get my civvy clothes on
No more soldiering for me!
When I leave the bloody Army
I won't need a weekend pass.
You can tell the Sergeant-Major
He can stuff it up his ———.

J A song from late 1915.
I want to go home, I want to go home.
I don't want to go to the trenches no more,
Where whizzbangs and   shrapnel   they whistle and roar,
Take me over the sea
Where the Germans can't get at me.
Oh my, I don't want to die,
I want to go home.

K There were plenty of references to fighting . . .
Gassed last night and gassed the night before,
Going to get gassed tonight if we never get gassed any more.
When we're gassed we're sick as we can be,
'Cos phosgene and mustard gas is much too much for me.
They're warning us, they're warning us,
One respirator for the four of us.
Thank your lucky stars that three of us can run,
So one of us can use it all alone.

Bombed last night and bombed the night before,
Going to get bombed tonight if we never get bombed any more.
When we're bombed we're scared as we can be.
God strafe the bombing planes from High Germany.
They're over us, they're over us,
One shell-hole for just the four of us,
Thank your lucky stars there are no more of us,
'Cos one of us could fill it all alone.

L . . . and officers.
Forward Joe Soap's army, marching without fear,
With our old commander, safely in the rear.
He boasts and   skites   from morn till night,
And thinks he's very brave,
But the men who really did the job are dead and in their grave.

Forward Joe Soap's army, marching without fear,
With our old commander, safely in the rear.

The wartime songs do not all give the same impression of the war. This partly depends on who wrote them and when they were written.

Read all the sources before answering the questions.
1 a) What was the soldiers' attitude to Ivor Novello (source D)?
b) Why do you think they preferred the cigarettes to his song?
c) His song was popular. What does that tell you about civilian attitudes to the war in 1914?
2 a) Look at sources B, E and F. What idea of the war do they give?
b) What do sources H, I and J have in common?
c) Which songs express dissatisfaction with the war? Explain your answer.
3 a) Please work in pairs. One of you writes about the attitudes to the war shown in sources B and F. The other writes about the attitudes shown in sources, I, J and K.
b) Compare your accounts. What differences do you notice? Give reasons for them.

A Posters told people not to waste scarce resources.

The Great War was the first in history to affect all the British people, even those who stayed at home. Life changed quite rapidly. The government passed the Defence of the Realm Act (DORA) in August 1914. It gave the government greater power over people's lives than ever before.

People could be told where to work; the railways and coal-mines were taken over by the government because they were essential to the war effort. British Summer Time was introduced: clocks went forward an hour to provide more daylight working hours. In 1916, Bank Holidays were cancelled. So was Bonfire Night.

DORA affected people's lives in many minor ways, too. Pub opening hours were cut and the beer was watered down. It was forbidden to buy someone else a drink – or to feed bread to an animal. It even restricted the kind of kite you could fly.

People eagerly read the newspapers to find out what was happening in the war. They scanned casualty lists for news of friends. But the newspapers were censored. The French army's dreadful losses in 1914 were hidden from the public. So was the loss of a British battleship in October 1914.

On the other hand, the public was bombarded with propaganda. Some of it was designed to whip up hatred of the German army. The public soon came to hate all things German – and that included Germans living in Britain. Even dachshund dogs were stoned in the streets.

The working class benefited from the war. By 1918, real incomes had risen by 20 per cent. Meanwhile, the average working week had dropped from 55 hours to 48 hours. But the rich found they had to do without servants: the men had gone to fight and the women often found war work.

Yet newspaper advertisements still offered holidays on the French Riviera. And, while the soldiers crossed the English Channel to fight in France, some of the rich were making the same journey – on holiday.

B A London crowd attacks a German-owned shop.

C The trenches came to Britain! People paid to visit these ones in Heaton Park, Manchester (1916). They were specially built to educate the public.

The Great War had many consequences for the British people. Some were more important than others. However, we must remember that the consequences for each person would vary. What was important for one might be less important for others.

D Arthur Blair: *Christmas Cards for the Collector* (1986).

For some months after the [start of war] the sending of greeting cards was banned by the Government for security reasons and to save paper 'essential to the war effort'. Then it was realized that Christmas and other cards were essential as a morale booster. So the Government allowed card manufacturers to have a quota of paper for the production of cards, once they realized their propaganda value.

Oct 24th

Orkney under martial law, all the windows facing Scapa got to be darkened at night; also all those facing the sea at Kirkwall + nobody allowed along the sea-front after dark (which rule is often broken by the way) The streets are very poorly lighted up + as for the lanes + back streets there's not lighted at all. As a result of all this darkness there's no comfort in walking out after dark, as the streets are crowded with coal-heavers, territorials &c.

30th American liner brought into Kirkwall Bay with some Germans aboard who were taken ashore as prisoners of war. Underneath the general cargo were hidden away 80 tons of rubber. contraband.

E A page from a young girl's diary for October 1914.

F Robert Roberts grew up in the slums of Salford. He described how the war affected slum children in *The Classic Slum* (1971).

By late 1916 children looked better fed. There were far fewer prosecutions for child neglect. Well before the end of the war the number of pupils taking free dinners at our school fell to one-fifth of the pre-1914 figures. Clogs and shawls generally began to give way to coats and hats, a sign of increasing affluence.

G Renee Huggett: *Growing up in the First World War* (1985).

The supply of toys in the shops [went down] during the war. The *Hampshire Telegraph and Post* reported on 28 December 1917 that there were no toys in Handley's winter sale in Southsea.

1 a) List all the consequences of the war which you can find. There are some in the text and others in the sources.
b) Which ones were economic consequences?
c) Which ones were social consequences?

2 a) Look through the consequences again. Pick out those which you think were most important for Britain. Give reasons for your choices.
b) Now, pick out those which were most important for (i) workers and (ii) children.
c) Which consequences most affected the rich? Explain how you decided.
d) Would the same consequences have affected the poor? Explain how you decided.
e) What evidence is there that some people were better-off as a result of the war?

WOMEN AND THE WAR

Before the war, women had been campaigning to get the vote. When war started, they stopped their protests. Instead, they handed out white feathers to the men to encourage them to go and fight. As more men joined up, businesses found themselves short of workers. So women took over the jobs which the men had left behind.

Some took over their husband's job: there were female blacksmiths and even grave-diggers. Others took over jobs directly linked to the war, such as driving an ambulance or nursing. About 25,000 women actually worked at the front. Far more went to work in banks, offices and, especially, factories. In many cases, they did jobs which women rarely did before 1914.

About 60 per cent of shell workers were women, often working a 70-hour week in dangerous conditions. A female munitions worker earned more than a soldier at the front – but only about half what a male shell worker was paid.

In most jobs, women earned less than men would earn for doing the same job. Some people said it was wrong to pay a single woman the same money as a man with a family to support.

During the war, over a million more women were doing paid work than before it. Many gave up working as servants or doing other low-paid work. The average wage for a working-class woman went up from 55p a week to £1.25 between 1914 and 1919.

Rich women, too, found their lives were quite different. Before the war, their social life was limited; fashionable long dresses over a tight corset meant that a day's work was impossible. The war gave them the chance to do something useful. Clothes became looser and skirts grew shorter.

Most women were delighted to make new friends and learn new skills. Others were pleased to give up working when the war was over. Many had no choice. Some trades unions made agreements with employers that the men would have their jobs back when they came home.

Yet the war had had its effect. 'We are different people,' wrote one woman in 1918. 'The people we were in 1914, we have lost sight of.'

A This reconstruction shows some of the jobs which women did in the war. The models are dressed as a shell worker, policewoman, nurse, railway ticket collector, member of the Women's Royal Naval Service, Land Army worker and Motor Drivers Corps volunteer.

B Women working in a shell factory.

C David Evans: *The Great War 1914-1918* (1981).
This was the start of a major social change. Before the war, women had been expected to marry and content themselves with family life and domestic work. Then it was considered   unbecoming   for a woman to work; now it was considered unpatriotic not to!

D Sarah Davies: *The Home Front* (1976).
For the first time women broke through the barriers which had confined them to their homes.

E Dudley Woodget: *World War I* (1976).
One of the most revolutionary changes of the war was the participation of women in the war effort. The upper-class women benefited most by being freed from [a pointless] life of tea-parties and gossip.

   The war gave women the chance to use their abilities and to obtain equality as citizens. In Britain they obtained in 1918 the vote for women over 30.

G The British were not keen on women working near their front line but this British nurse is seen at a Belgian artillery position in 1914.

The Great War brought many changes in women's lives but this does not mean that every woman's life changed in the same way. We must be very careful when making general statements about changes.

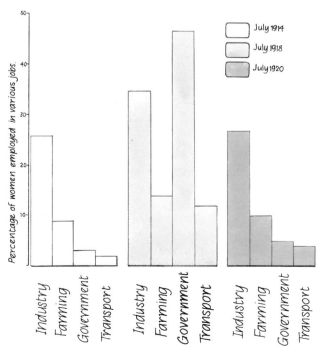

F The percentage of female workers in various industries, 1914-20.

1 a) Look at source A. From the left, write down what job each woman was doing.
   b) This picture is a reconstruction. Does that mean that it is less reliable than source G? Explain your answer.
2 a) How did life change for rich women?
   b) How did life change for poor women?
   c) Were these rapid or gradual changes? Give a reason.
3 a) What consequences did the war have for women?
   b) Which consequences were long term and which were short term? Explain how you decided.
   c) Read sources C and D carefully. Do you think these are good accounts of what happened? Give reasons.
4 a) What changes took place, according to source F?
   b) Give reasons for the different figures on the three dates.
   c) Does this source show that women made progress during 1914-20? Explain your answer carefully.

MEDICINE AND HEALTH

War brought great progress in medicine. One of the killer diseases of 1914 was tetanus, which was caused by infected wounds. Sleeping on muddy ground made infection more likely.

In the third month of the war, one in every 30 wounded soldiers developed tetanus. So all men who were wounded were immediately injected with tetanus serum. In the following month, only one wounded soldier in 600 caught the disease.

Carrying out operations had always been difficult because patients lost blood during the operation. In 1915, doctors discovered a chemical which stopped blood from clotting. This meant that blood could now be stored to use later and blood transfusions were successfully carried out.

Scientists solved another problem. Lice spread rapidly in the trenches. During the war, doctors discovered that it was lice which caused typhus fever. They were also one of the causes of a new disease, trench fever.

There were general improvements in health, too. In 1914, more than one in 10 babies died before their first birthday. The government tried hard to reduce this high death rate.

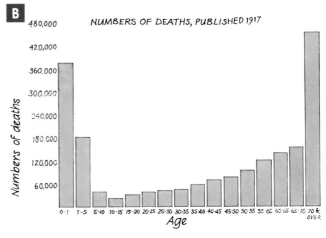

B   NUMBERS OF DEATHS, PUBLISHED 1917

In 1917, the first National Baby Week was held. Parades of mothers with prams marched through the nation's towns. By 1919, infant deaths had fallen.

People were better paid and they ate better. Many poor children were better fed than ever before. In poorer areas, food kitchens were set up. Mostly, they served penny portions of food, mainly to children and old age pensioners. One kitchen even offered dinner for six for just 5p. This was what you got:

Naval blockades reduced food imports and food prices went up. But food only became scarce later in the war. White bread was banned in 1916 because grain was in short supply. In 1917, people were asked to eat only 1.1 kg of meat a week. It hardly affected the poor: they ate less than this anyway.

But the government was not keen to introduce rationing. This meant that the rich could always buy food easily while the poor began queuing before dawn to get their share. There were such protests that, in the end, the government had to act. On 1 January, 1918, sugar was rationed. By the spring, butter, tea, jam, margarine, meat and bacon had been added to the ration list.

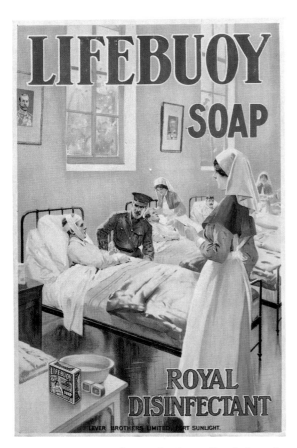

A   Yet another firm which realised that the war could sell products was Lifebuoy Soap.

C Second Lieutenant Chapman wrote home from France in May 1917.

Shall we have MEATLESS DAYS? If so, I think I will stay out here! Today we have had new potatoes, and fresh cauliflower! And I have drunk red wine of the best. If I come home shall I have to dig potatoes? What a terrible place England is getting. I hope the war will stop soon, to prevent it getting any worse.

D The Public Meals Order of January 1918 included these restrictions.

Two days each week shall be meatless. (Tuesday and Friday in London; Wednesday and Friday elsewhere.)
No meat shall be served for breakfast.
Fats to be rationed.
People over ten may only drink milk in hot drinks.
Guests must bring their own sugar with them, unless staying in hotels.
Not more than 1.5 ozs [42g] of bread, cake, scone or biscuit may be served for afternoon tea.

E From the diary of Reverend Andrew Clark (1917).

In some of the cottages very little food is taken except bread. Cottagers are terribly alarmed as to what will happen if they are put on fixed weight of bread. One family of seven uses [14.5kg] of loaves each week. Under the official scale this household would be allowed only [12.6kg] per week.

F The French Red Cross at work in the war.

It is essential to ask questions about sources before relying on them. Each of the sources on this page is genuine but the evidence they give may be misleading.

1 a) Read the first column. What medical changes happened during the war?
b) Look at source A. How would this scene be (i) different and (ii) similar today?
c) How reliable do you think source A is? Give reasons.
d) What can you still learn from source A?

2 a) Look at source F. If this incident happened today, what would be (i) different and (ii) similar about it?
b) How reliable do you think source F is? Give reasons.
c) What can you still learn from source F?

3 a) What would you need to know about source E before you relied on it? Give reasons.
b) 'Source C gives a typical picture of life in the trenches.' Do you agree? Explain your answer.

INDUSTRY AND WAR

A A female munitions worker working on a gun barrel at Woolwich Arsenal.

When war began, British industry was just not organised to cope with its demands. For goods such as chemicals, the country relied on imports from the United States and Germany. Britain could not even produce all the munitions which were needed.

Step by step, the government worked to change this situation. In 1915, it passed the Munitions Act. At a stroke, it put Britain's industry on a war footing. By 1917, more ammunition was leaving Britain in one week than had been produced in the whole 30 years before the war.

The Act limited the profits which businesses could make. Union rules were suspended if they got in the way of producing goods. Strikes could be banned and disputes had to be settled by arbitration. In effect, workers in munition industries had to stay in their jobs until war was over.

However, other problems remained. Britain needed better machine tools to make the machines which would make the goods. The United States provided both the machine tools and the know-how of mass production. And, in 1916, she provided most of the shells used by Britain in battles like the one on the River Somme.

By the end of the war, the government had huge powers to control industry. Some of the changes it made were lasting, as with the railways. Before the war, there were 130 separate railway companies. The government took over the whole lot. In 1921, the system was re-organised under just four companies.

In other industries, the effects were less lasting. Although the government took over the coal mines in 1916, there were no great technical improvements. Nor did productivity increase: in fact, production fell towards the end of the war. And there were bitter and frequent strikes.

Throughout the war, it was illegal to sell goods to the enemy – but the trade still went on. Industry got round the laws by selling goods to a neutral country which then sold them to the enemy. In this way, Russian metal was sold to Germany; France supplied Germany with fodder and cattle. Pathé, the French film-maker, used German film which he bought from the United States. Amazingly, German businessmen even sold shells to the enemy.

B An official British postcard, possibly for use in the United States.

C These female gas-workers are pushing barrows of coke (1916).

D C J Pennethorne Hughes described trade between the enemies in *The Nineteenth Century and the World War* (1935).

All through the war the great armament firms were supplied from the enemy countries. The French and the British sold war materials to the Germans through Switzerland [and other neutral countries]. The Germans supplied optical sights, it is said, for the British Admiralty. The armament industry, which had helped stimulate the war, made millions out of it.

E Marc Ferro described British trade to Germany in *The Great War 1914-1918* (1973).

[The] British attaché in Denmark reckoned that Holland had imported twelve times as much cocoa during the years 1914-1918 as during the years 1910-14, while her exports to Germany rose virtually in the same proportion. Cotton was the same, as were fish, rubber and other essential goods. In England and at the front there were shortages, for instance of motor-oil; the same goods were going from England to Sweden, Denmark and then Germany.

F David Watson fought in a Scottish Battalion at the Somme. He described a captured German trench.

We found dugouts made of solid concrete, [with] electric light and carpeted with British cement bags. The cement bags annoyed me for a long time. Somebody was making money out of it.

G Female worker on the shell production line.

Pictures must be very carefully studied to discover how reliable they are. This often means that the historian needs background information about the pictures. Sometimes, there are doubts about pictures but this does not stop us learning a great deal from them.

Study all the pictures carefully.

1 a) Which one is obviously propaganda? Explain how you know.
   b) What can we learn from this source?

2 a) What can you learn from source C?
   b) Source C was included in a recruitment booklet in 1916. Now that you know that, what else can you learn from this source?
   c) Compare the clothing of the women in sources A and G. What difference do you notice?
   d) Look again at source A. Suggest a reason why the clothing differs.

3 a) List the consequences which the war had for industry. Write one on each line.
   b) Which of these consequences were social and which were economic? Write E for economic or S for social beside your answers to (a).
   c) Which do you think were most important? Give reasons.

1914	1915	1916	1917	1918	1919

A This German flyer shows an early method of dropping bombs on the enemy.

In 1914, aircraft were used mainly for reconnaissance . Pilots watched for signs of enemy troops moving up to the front lines; they took photographs of enemy trenches. These helped the artillery to select their targets.

At first, the air war was very gentlemanly: pilots saluted each other as they passed. But soon they were carrying rifles or pistols to shoot each other. Even so, there were relaxed moments. On 1 April 1915, one British plane dropped a football on the Germans as a joke.

By then, planes were fitted with machine-guns. But it was not easy flying a plane and firing a machine-gun; in any case, there was a risk that you might shoot your own propeller blades to bits. The man who solved the problem for the Germans was a Dutchman, Anthony Fokker.

He managed to synchronise the machine-gun with the propeller blade. This allowed the pilot to fire *between* the blades every time. It turned the aircraft into a *fighting* machine. But it made life more dangerous for pilots: in 1916, the working life of a British pilot averaged just three weeks.

Another development was bombing. Enemy trenches were one target but both Germans and British bombed other targets, including cities. The first German raid on Britain was as early as January 1915; it was the first time that civilians had ever been bombed from the air.

At first, these raids were made by zeppelins. These were huge airships, filled with hydrogen gas. Altogether, there were 51 zeppelin raids on Britain; they caused about 1,900 casualties, including 564 deaths. One British newspaper called them 'baby-killing machines'.

New means of attack led inevitably to new means of defence. Anti-aircraft guns were improved. Barrage balloons were strung across the sky and searchlights were used to light up a zeppelin, making it an easier target. Explosive bullets were used to set the hydrogen on fire; once ablaze, they were death traps.

B Panic in Britain: a German postcard of 1916 shows the effect they hoped zeppelin raids would have.

E Sybil Morrison watched the end of another zeppelin in September 1916. Afterwards, she became a pacifist. Years later, she described it.

To me, it was an awful sight. All of the bag part had caught fire. We knew that there were about sixty people in it and that they were being roasted to death. I was appalled to see the kind, good-hearted British people dancing about in the streets – clapping and singing and cheering. When I said I was appalled that anyone could be pleased to see such a terrible sight they said, 'But they're Germans; they're the enemy' – not human beings. I turned my back on it; I suddenly thought it's not right. It is wrong and I can't have any further part in it.

F VS Pritchett recalled seeing bomber planes over London in *A Cab at the Door* (1968).

It was, for those days, startling. A flight of aircraft had bombed London for the first time by day. I saw the street walls of several houses had been stripped off, carts were overturned and horses lay dead among the crowds. The pubs in Bermondsey had filled with women pouring drink into themselves and their babies as I left.

G Sylvia Pankhurst described Londoners' reactions in *The Home Front* (1932).

When the police gave the official warning, the underground railways and cellars were open to the people. Great crowds flocked [there], often half-dressed, carrying their children, and laden with rugs and pillows and things most precious to them. As the terror grew, families ceased to wait for the warning, and camped out nightly on the pavements outside the closed doors of the tubes. A panic took place on one occasion, and people were killed by the press of others crowding behind them.

C This painting shows the end of a zeppelin. It was about as long as 2½ football pitches.

So the Germans switched to using Gotha bombers. In 1918, they killed over 800 people and caused great panic. Meanwhile, the British had been attacking German cities. In 1916, British and French attacks on Karlsruhe killed or wounded 26 women and 124 children. The British public, of course, was not told.

Aircraft development had been rapid during the war. In August 1914, the Royal Flying Corps had taken just 37 planes to France. In 1918, Britain` ended the war with 22,000 planes – the biggest airforce in the world.

D Colonel Arthur Borton recorded the destruction of a zeppelin in his diary (1 April 1916).

Joyful news.
A Zeppelin brought down last night in flames by our anti-aircraft gunners.

_1 a) Read the text. What changes took place during the war?
b) For each change, suggest at least one reason why it happened.
c) Pick any two of these changes and explain what consequences they had.

_2 a) What can you learn from source A?
b) Do you think it shows a real bombing raid or not? Explain your view.
c) Does your answer to (b) mean that this source is not reliable? Explain carefully.

_3 a) Read sources D and E. How do the two people's attitudes differ?
b) Why were most people pleased that zeppelins were destroyed? Answer in detail.
c) You are Sybil Morrison. Write a postcard to a friend describing what you saw and your feelings about it.
d) Now, write a postcard as if you were one of the people who had been dancing in the street.

MORE NEW TECHNOLOGY

1914	1915	1916	1917	1918	1919

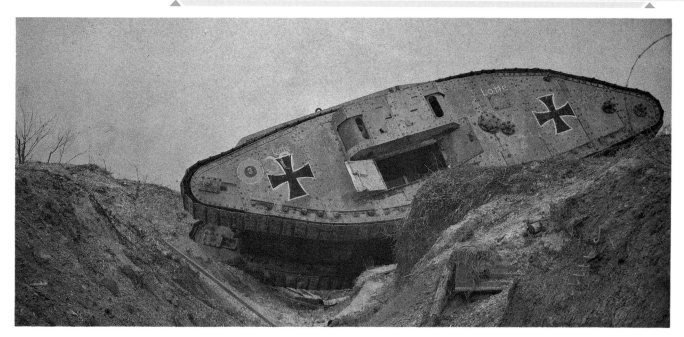

A Photograph of a tank with German markings (1918).

One of the jobs of industry was to develop new weapons. As time passed, each side hoped to find a new weapon which would end the war quickly. Neither side succeeded.

In July 1917, British troops were faced with a new German weapon, although it was first made by a British chemist. It was mustard gas. It burns the skin, damages the lungs and can cause blindness.

By 1918, about one shell in four being fired on the Western Front contained gas. In all, there were over one million gas casualties during the war. But neither side really believed that gas would break the deadlock in the trenches. It was seen as a useful 'accessory', which was what soldiers called it. The generals had higher hopes for the war's other new weapon – the tank.

As early as 1914, Ernest Swinton of the Royal Engineers had seen that tanks might break through enemy lines in a way that men could not. They would not be affected by machine-gun fire, they would cut through enemy wire and drive straight over trenches.

The new weapon was secret. This caused something of a problem: it was just too large to hide. So it was given the code name 'tank' because its body looked like a large water tank.

Tanks were first used at the Somme on 15 September 1916. There were few of them and they made little impact. But Haig was impressed and wanted 1,000 of them quickly. Yet it was November 1917 before there was a mass tank attack at Cambrai – and then the cavalry follow-up was a failure.

The Germans were slow to realise how useful the tank could be. It was spring 1918 before they had tanks in battle and they did not perform well. The biggest Allied tank attack came late in the war, in August 1918, when enemy lines were broken. By then, the war was nearly over.

B Tank production, 1916-18.

	heavy	medium	light
G. B.	2,917	281	
France		800	3,500
Germany	20		

The first tanks

C Major Trevor wrote about tanks to his parents on 16 September 1916 during the Battle of the Somme.

We have had great news this morning which I suppose you will see in tomorrow's papers. We seem to be doing splendidly. Our new implement of war seems to have thoroughly frightened the Hun. I do hope we shall break through and am beginning to feel quite confident.

D Robert Hoare described events on 15 September 1916 in *World War One* (1973).

In No Man's Land were 24 metal monsters moving on tracks. They were the first tanks to be used in the history of warfare.

E British troops surrounding one of the tanks used on 15 September.

F *The American Heritage History of World War One* (1964).

[Tanks] should have been stock-piled for the staging of a monster surprise. But Haig's desire to bull through was too great. He grabbed the first forty-two and threw them into an attack on September 15. The effects were sensational. The rumbling monsters seemed to scare German infantrymen out of their wits.

G David Evans wrote about the same event in *The Great War 1914-18* (1981).

During the battle the tank was used for the first time. Haig had only fifty of these at the start of the battle. He was advised not to use them until they were available in greater numbers. The British commander ignored the [advice] and on 15 September 1916 the first tanks went into action. Sadly, twenty-eight broke down before they reached the battle area. The remaining thirty-two scurried into the mud and were soon bogged down or knocked out. The trial run was a failure.

H This British poster was printed to raise money to build more tanks.

1   a) Describe what you can see in source A.
    b) The photograph shows a *British* tank. How, then, do you explain the caption?
    c) What can you learn from this about using photographs as evidence?

2   a) Read all the sources. How do sources D, F and G disagree?
    b) Read source G *very carefully*. Why would a historian be unwise to rely on this source?
    c) How do D and G agree?
    d) How do sources F and G agree?

3   a) What opinions are given in (i) source C and (ii) source G?
    b) How do sources C and G disagree?
    c) Suggest reasons why they disagree.
    d) Discuss the weakness and strengths of sources C and G.
    e) Major Trevor thought they were 'doing splendidly'. Why would his circumstances cause him to make this judgement? Explain carefully.

A The battlefield of Ypres. 'Good God, did we really send men to fight in that?' asked Haig's Chief-of-Staff when he saw the scene afterwards.

Meanwhile, the attempts to break the deadlock went on. In April 1917, the French General Nivelle launched an attack to break through enemy lines. He planned to advance six miles (10km) on the first day; the best they managed was just one (1.6km).

As the fighting went on, there were serious mutinies in the French army. Parts of the front were not even defended – but the Germans didn't know. Nor did the British public: they were not told of the mutinies.

In July, it was the turn of the British. Yet another attack was planned at Ypres. For 10 days beforehand, the British shelled the Germans: in all, over four million shells were fired. (They cost £20 million.) The main effect was to destroy the drainage system.

To make matters worse, it was a wet summer. In August alone, there was twice as much rain as usual. The results were awful. Tanks sank in the mud. Men slipped off muddy duckboards and drowned in shell holes full of clinging mud. The living sometimes drank water from shell holes which contained rotting corpses.

Back in Britain, the newspapers told the public how well the battle was going. But on the battlefield it took 16 men to carry a stretcher normally carried by just two. They were under instructions to leave anyone who was seriously injured.

But Haig would not give up. In October, he launched a new phase of the attack – to capture the little village of Passchendaele. By the time Canadian troops got there in November it was mostly rubble. A few days later, the offensive ended. The Allies had advanced just five miles (8 km) and gained Passchendaele. Five months later, the Germans recaptured it.

B From the journal of Private Ernest Atkins.
Not a tree, not a blade of grass, not a bird, not an insect – one vast stretch of poisoned earth and mud. No one can imagine such a place unless they had actually seen it. The effect on you was worse than shelling or fighting, although you had that as well. Will power alone kept you going. Once lose that and you were finished.

C Private Reg Lawrence described his experiences in November.

We passed two Germans (they were hardly more than 17 years of age) clinging to each other and weeping, unable to move apparently. I signed to them to go back with the prisoners, but they could only stare and moan. [They were] completely broken by the terrific blast of shell fire that had passed over them . . .

Of our Company only thirty-two men answered roll call. Puckrin has shell shock. Engels' leg is broken by a shell. Hands is wounded. Roscoe is dead. I am the last and I have no companions left.

I see no excuse for war, unless it is in defence of home and dear ones. Otherwise it is just legalised murder on a large scale. In war you murder a man you have never seen, who has never done you an injury. How absurd!

D Hugh Quigley: *A Diary of 1917* (published in 1928).

The country resembles a sewage-heap more than anything else, pitted with shell holes, and filled with green, slimy water. Above [them] a blackened arm or leg might [stick up]. It becomes a matter of great skill picking a way across such a network of death-traps. Drowning is almost certain in one of them.

E This view of the scene around Ypres was painted by Paul Nash. He called it *We Are Making a New World*.

F When it was over; a Canadian machine-gun crew at Passchendaele in November.

G The German General Ludendorff later wrote this.

Enormous masses of ammunition were hurled upon men who spent a miserable existence scattered about in mud-filled shell holes. It was no longer life at all. It was mere unspeakable suffering.

All sources are useful. But some are more useful than others for a particular task. We have both photographs and paintings of the Great War. Historians must decide what they want to learn from their sources, then decide which sources are most useful for answering their questions.

1 a) What can you learn from the painting about the battlefield?
b) What can you learn from the photographs about the battlefield?
c) Which kind of source is more useful for understanding the conditions in which men fought? Give reasons.
d) Read the title of Paul Nash's painting. What do you think his opinion was of the fighting? Explain how you decided.

2 a) Why was it hard for the British public to find out the truth about the battle?
b) Why would it have been hard for ordinary soldiers to know what was happening?
c) Does that mean that secondary sources about the battle are more useful than primary sources? Give careful reasons.

THE WAR IN POETRY

Today, many pupils study poems about the war as part of their English course. In one sense, it's easy to study war poets; there were so many of them. One writer has listed 2,225 people who had poems published between 1914 and 1918. At least 532 of them were women. And this number does not include all those who had poems published in papers and magazines.

Yet these studies can be misleading. Wilfred Owen and Siegfried Sassoon are two of the poets often studied today. Yet Owen was unknown at the time and Sassoon was not widely read. The most popular poet of the day was John Oxenham: today, he is usually ignored.

Collections of poetry can mislead in another way. Often, they are organised so that the reader thinks that attitudes changed during the war. The early poems of 1914-15 are optimistic: men bravely go off to fight, with great hopes for the future.

Later poems show how bitter the soldiers became, once they knew what the trenches were like. The optimism is gone. War has hardened them. Then, finally, come the protest poems and demands that there should be nothing like it ever again.

It just shows how you can select sources to prove whatever you want. The truth is that you can find 'realistic' poems from early in the war – and you can find optimistic poems from 1918. It all depends what you are looking for.

Books tend to print poems by famous writers, but you can find these easily in your school library. So we have mostly chosen poems by unknown poets. As you read them, ask yourself what they tell us about people's attitudes towards the war.

A *Little Folks* was quick off the mark with this advice for Christmas 1914.

Little girls and little boys,
Never suck your German toys;
German soldiers licked will make
Darling Baby's tummy ache.

Parents, you should always try
Only British toys to buy;
Though to pieces they be picked,
British soldiers can't be licked.

B Picture postcards (right) often included predictable poems.

C A poem by H H Munro who was killed on the Western Front in 1916.

While shepherds watched their flocks by night
All seated on the ground,
A high-explosive shell came down
And mutton rained around.

D A poem by CSM Sidney Chaplin.

You stand in a trench of vile stinking mud
And the bitter cold wind freezes your blood
Then the guns open up and flames light the sky
And, as you watch, rats go scuttling by.

The men in the dugouts are quiet for a time
Trying to sleep midst the stench and the slime
The moon is just showing from over the Hill
And the dead on the wire hang silent and still.

A sniper's bullet wings close to your head
As you wistfully think of a comfortable bed
But now a dirty blanket has to suffice
And more often than not it is crawling with lice.

Haig and his mob keep well in the Rear,
Living in luxury, safe in old St Omer,
Flashing Red Tabs, Brass and Ribbons Galore,
What the hell do they know about fighting a war?

Let not Invasion scares or Bombs from Zeppelins drive you balmy — There's naught can harm old Britain now for *I* have joined the Army!

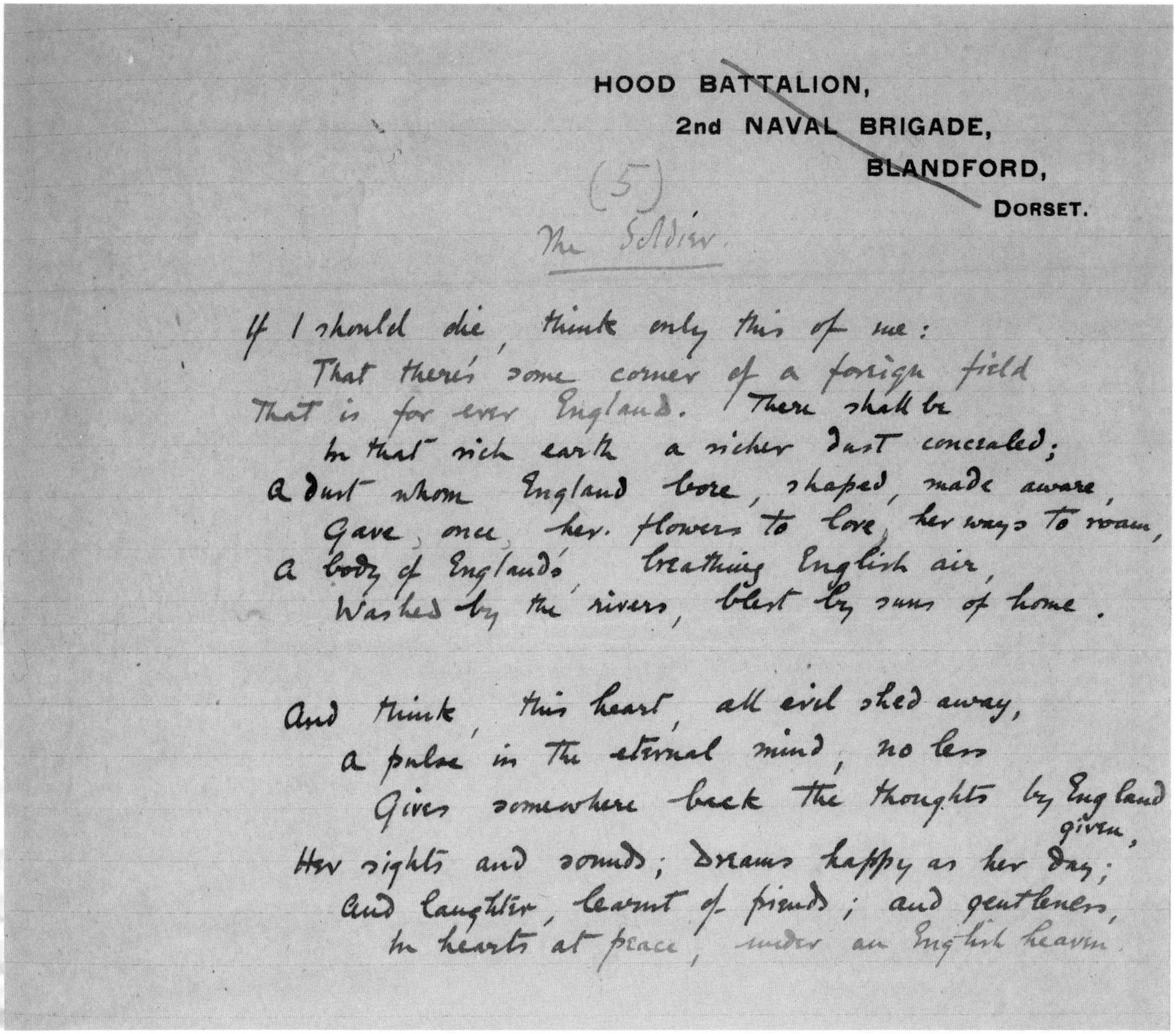

HOOD BATTALION,
2nd NAVAL BRIGADE,
BLANDFORD,
DORSET.

(5)

The Soldier.

If I should die, think only this of me:
That there's some corner of a foreign field
That is for ever England. There shall be
In that rich earth a richer dust concealed;
A dust whom England bore, shaped, made aware,
Gave, once, her flowers to love, her ways to roam,
A body of England's, breathing English air,
Washed by the rivers, blest by suns of home.

And think, this heart, all evil shed away,
A pulse in the eternal mind, no less
Gives somewhere back the thoughts by England given,
Her sights and sounds; dreams happy as her day;
And laughter, learnt of friends; and gentleness,
In hearts at peace, under an English heaven.

E The manuscript of *The Soldier* by Rupert Brooke (December 1914). First published in 1915, Brooke's poems stayed popular throughout the war.

F Some verses from *The Battalion ABC*, printed in a newspaper of the 5th Gloucesters (1915).

C. stands for Chelmsford, the town of our training,
And where it is almost continually raining.
D. is the word which all of us said
When the billets were changed and we hadn't a bed.
E. is for England, now distant and dear.
When we see her white cliffs again, how we will cheer.

G This poem appeared in a service newspaper (1918).

It's a long road that has no turning
It's never 'too late' to mend;
The darkest hour is before the dawn
And *even this* war must end.

1 Explain why a collection of poems might give misleading ideas about the war.

2 a) Which of these poems is propaganda? Explain how you decided.
b) Which aspects of trench life are described in source D?
c) Which aspects are missing?
d) What can you learn about soldiers' attitudes from these poems?
e) Which poem do you think best shows how soldiers felt about the war? Give reasons for your choice.
f) 'These are mostly poor poems so they are no real use as sources.' Explain whether you agree or disagree.

3 Read source F. Make up more verses for this poem about other aspects of life in the war.

A This German postcard showed U-boat sinkings from February 1917 to January 1918.

February, Germany announced that any ship in the eastern Atlantic Ocean would be sunk. Almost at once, the U-Boats began attacking neutral ships. They included American ones.

But the policy was risky. Germany knew that it might cause the United States to join the war against her. That is exactly what happened. The USA declared war on Germany on 6 April 1917.

That same month, over one million tons of shipping were sunk. One in four ships leaving British ports was destroyed. Germany's policy very nearly worked: Britain had just six weeks' food supplies left. But, in May, the British government introduced the convoy system. This meant that merchant ships had to sail in groups while a Royal Navy vessel protected them. The convoy system cut losses dramatically.

Throughout the war, the British fleet blockaded enemy ports to stop food and raw materials from getting to them. German shoppers found some goods very hard to find. People drank coffee made from dandelion roots and barley; raspberry leaves were turned into tea. As the war drew to a close, it was the German people who faced starvation, not the British.

Britain had spent a fortune on its dreadnoughts. They fought just one major battle. In May 1916, the British Grand Fleet set sail from its Scottish base and met the German High Seas Fleet off the Danish coast. The British called it the Battle of Jutland; the Germans called it Skagerrak.

The Kaiser said that the Germans won. The British lost 14 ships; the Germans lost 11. Over 6,000 British sailors died compared with 2,500 Germans. But the German fleet did not risk another battle during the rest of the war.

In fact, what worried the British government were not the enemy's dreadnoughts but its U-boats. Although Britain began the war with more submarines, Germany increased its U-boat fleet from 20 in 1914 to nearly 200 in 1918.

Amongst the ships sunk by U-Boats in 1915 was a liner called the *Lusitania*. The event caused great anger in the United States because the dead included 124 Americans.

In 1917, Germany planned to use its U-Boats to end the war quickly: they would sink merchant ships and starve Britain into giving up. In

B This British postcard reminded people that the German navy played little part after Jutland.

C Two newspaper headlines about the Battle of Jutland.
The German High Seas Fleet ran away. (British newspaper)
The German fleet has assaulted its jailor, but is still in jail. (American newspaper)

GROWING TOLL OF ENEMY LOSSES IN THE SEA BATTLE

Majority of the German Light Cruisers and Destroyers Reported Lost.

FLOTILLA DRIVEN INTO THEIR OWN MINEFIELD

How Airships and Airmen Scouts Helped the German Fleet—20 Torpedo Boats Gone.

THREE ZEPPELINS BROUGHT DOWN.

Only two brief official communiqués on the North Sea battle were issued last night. Neither adds anything further to the details of the fight.

One corrects German lies about our losses and the other gives a brief summary of our casualties among officers. Admiral Beatty is reported to be unharmed.

A dramatic statement last night was that the German destroyer and light cruiser flotilla were driven into their own minefield and the majority of them lost. German survivors speak of at least twenty torpedo craft as among their "colossal" losses.

The outstanding fact is that the German Fleet—"the whole German fleet"—emerged from its Canal on "an enterprise directed towards the North." It failed in its purpose; and when the British "main forces" appeared on the scene, fled back to its base.

Yesterday three Zeppelins were reported destroyed in the battle—two shot down over the sea and one wrecked just as she got back to Germany.

"WE ARE THE GAINERS."

Mr. Churchill on the Admirals' Reports on the Sea Fight.

THE BLOW TO THE ENEMY.

Mr. Winston Churchill, who has had the privilege of examining the reports of the admirals and of considering the information in the possession of the Admiralty, says:—

"The naval supremacy of the British Fleet in capital ships depends upon the super-Dreadnoughts armed with the 13.5in. and 15in. guns, and these are sufficient by themselves to maintain control of the seas.

"Of these vital units of the first rank we have only lost one—the Queen Mary. There appears to be no doubt that the Germans have lost at least one comparable ship.

"If this should be the Lutzow or the Derfflinger, that vessel is the heavier loss to them, actually and relatively, than the Queen Mary is to us.

"The sinking of the two brand new German light cruisers, Wiesbaden and Elbing, is, in fact, a more grievous loss to the enemy. In all those vessels the most serious feature is the loss of their splendid and irreplacable crews.

"The destroyer casualties appear to be about equal. On these terms, we, being the stronger, are the gainers.

"Our margin of superiority is in no way impaired. The dispatch of troops to the Con-

OUR LINE PIERCED IN BIG ATTACK.

Germans' 700 Yards Gain on Ypres Front.

TWO GENERALS MISSING.

Canadian Counter-Attacks Regain Much Lost Ground.

(BRITISH OFFICIAL.)

GENERAL HEADQUARTERS, Saturday, 10.19 p.m.

Fighting of a very severe nature has continued without cessation south-east of Ypres, between Hooge and Ypres-Menin Railway.

Following on their initial advantage obtained yesterday evening in penetrating our forward line in this neighbourhood, the Germans pushed their attacks during the night and succeeded in pushing through our defences to a depth of 700 yards in the direction of Zillebeke.

The Canadian troops, however, who are holding this sector of the defences, launched counter-strokes at 7 a.m. this morning which have succeeded gradually in driving the enemy from much of the ground which he had gained.

The Canadians behaved with the utmost gallantry in counter-attacking successfully after a heavy and continuous bombardment.

The enemy losses have been severe, and a

D The headline from a British newspaper four days after the battle.

E Nigel Kelly: *The First World War* (1989).
The Kaiser argued that the British fleet had finally been defeated; but, since the German fleet never emerged from port again, the British claimed victory. It was a battle both sides could claim to have won.

F *The American Heritage History of World War 1* (1964).
Jutland gave no cheer to England. If not a defeat, it was a [disastrous] victory. The [German] High Seas Fleet had struck down 117,025 tons of British warships; the Grand Fleet had sunk about 61,180 tons of German naval power. German armor had stood up better; German gunnery had shown itself more accurate. Both sides claimed a triumph. The Germans did not again venture forth. For England, that was the only entry on the bright side.

G Corelli Barnett: *The Sword Bearers* (1963).
The Germans claimed a victory. Since the British had forced the Germans back into port, they too claimed a victory. British propaganda did its best for Jutland but it was a curious 'victory'. For forty years [people argued about] who was to blame for it.

FACTS OF THE SEA BATTLE

ADMIRAL BEATTY FIGHTS THE WHOLE GERMAN FLEET.

COMPENSATION FOR OUR HEAVY LOSS.

ADMIRALTY COUNTS 18 GERMAN SHIPS SUNK AGAINST OUR 14.

H A newspaper headline after the battle.

I Official German statement, June 1916.
The Kaiser addresses the crews of the High Seas Fleet: The British Fleet was beaten. The first great hammer blow was struck, and the [halo] of British world supremacy disappeared.

J Another historian's view (1988).
The Kaiser insisted on regarding the battle as a victory. He was quite wrong. Jellicoe [the commander of the British fleet] had not won a great victory, but he had not suffered a defeat. He remained ready to proceed to sea at four hours' notice. The Kaiser [was warned] that the High Seas Fleet needed a month to make good the damage it had suffered.

Interpretations of events often disagree. This may be because some primary sources are propaganda and do not seek to tell the whole truth. Secondary sources also differ. A historian's interpretation depends on judgements about primary sources. He or she chooses which ones are most reliable and important.

---

1 a) Why did Germany use U-Boats against British ships?
   b) What were the results of these actions in 1917?
   c) What action did the British government take as a result?

2 a) Read all the sources. Which sources are propaganda? Explain how you decided.
   b) Compare the sources with the text. Which one is incorrect? Explain how you decided.
   c) What evidence is there that the British came off worse than the Germans?
   d) What evidence is there that the Germans came off worse than the British?
   e) Did the writers of sources F and G think the British had won? Explain your answer carefully.
   f) What three interpretations of the battle do the sources give?
   g) Which interpretation do you think is best? Explain how you decided.

The United States joined the Allies in April 1917. But, in November, there was a revolution in Russia and the new leaders pulled Russia out of the war. Fighting ended on the Eastern Front. However, time was running out for Germany. The German generals knew they could not win once the Americans arrived. So, during the winter of 1917–18, they planned a last great offensive to break the Allied lines.

At first, it worked. By April, German troops were just 50 miles (80km) from Paris. German troops had found open ground beyond the trench network: at last, the armies were on the move once again. Source A shows Germans advancing in April past the corpse of a British soldier.

But it was the last gasp of an exhausted army. Supplies of food and ammunition simply could not keep up with the troops. German soldiers stopped to loot Allied food and drink – and the attack slowed down. They could see that German propaganda about poor Allied supplies was not true.

Meanwhile, the Allies had put their armies under the leadership of one man – General Foch. He counter-attacked and, by early August, the German forces were retreating. On 8 August, the German army was pushed back 7 miles (11km). General Ludendorff called it 'the blackest day for the German army'.

These were black days for the German people too. There were serious food shortages. Butcher's shops sold crows and a doctor's prescription was needed to get eggs. A typical day's food for an adult provided just 1,000 calories.

On 26 September, Allied troops broke through the Hindenburg Line – the last line of German defences. Just a week later, the German Chancellor asked the United States to arrange a ceasefire.

Now that they were winning, the Allies were in no hurry to agree peace terms. They carried on talking while Germany's allies collapsed. Bulgaria had made peace in September; in October, Turkey gave up. That same month, there was a mutiny in the German navy.

Early in November, it was all over. Riots broke out in Munich on 7 November; by 9 November, people were protesting in the streets of Berlin. That same day, the Kaiser abdicated and later fled to Holland.

The end came on 11 November 1918. At about 5a.m., an armistice was signed. Fighting would end at 11a.m., Paris time. That same morning, Canadian troops captured Mons – the same town where the British had first fought over four years earlier.

B Going home to mother; postcards were quick to celebrate the armistice.

C Sir Charles Petrie described the scenes in London on 11 November 1918.

I went to the Savoy [hotel] that evening and the first thing I saw was a girl in evening dress being sick in the gutter. Nobody minded or appeared to think it odd. Inside, young officers were trying to burn a German flag in spite of the protests of the management.

D Rifleman Harold Clegg was in hospital in England on 11 November.

The Matron entered with a telegram in her hand. It was a complete surprise to us to hear that the armistice had been signed. Somehow the news did not [mean] very much to us; the fact that the war had ended was news that had come too late; it mattered little to most of those seated in the dining hall whether the war finished or whether it continued for years. We had nothing to gain by its coming to an end; we were out of it for ever.

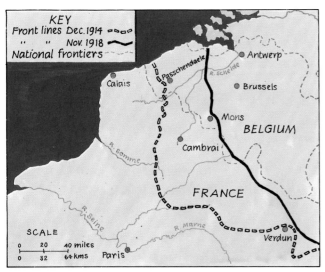

KEY
Front lines Dec. 1914 ⊙⊙⊙⊙
  " " Nov. 1918 ━━━
National frontiers

Antwerp
Calais
Passchendaele
R. Scheldt
Brussels
Mons
BELGIUM
Cambrai
R. Somme
FRANCE
R. Seine
R. Marne
Verdun
Paris

SCALE
0 20 40 miles
0 32 64 kms

E Where the war began and ended: the Western Front, 1914-18.

F Richard Collier: *The Plague of the Spanish Lady* (1974).

At Rossall School, near Fleetwood, a sick-bay of boys [with flu] received in glum silence the matron's news that the war was over. But later that day, she returned to announce, 'Boys, I regret to tell you your Headmaster has been stricken by the [flu]'. They cheered until the rafters rang.

G Colonel W N Nicholson remembered:

Just before 11 a.m., a thousand rounds were fired from [a German machine-gun opposite]. At five minutes to eleven the machine-gunner got up, took off his hat to us, and walked away. At 11 a.m., there came great cheering from the German lines; and the village church bells rang. But on our side there were only a few shouts. I had heard more for a rum ration. The match was over; it had been a damned bad game.

H Molly Macleod wrote to her mother on 12 November.

People had different feelings about the armistice. These depended on who they were and where they were at the time. It's not even true that everyone was pleased that war was over.

1 a) Why did the Germans plan a spring offensive?
b) What reasons are given for why the Germans gave up?
c) What primary sources would you need to prove that these were the real reasons?

2 a) Read all the sources. Write down all the different reactions to the armistice.
b) Suggest reasons why people did not all feel the same.
c) Which source do you think gives the best idea of how most people felt? Explain how you decided.
d) What would you need to know about sources F and G before you relied on them?

THE COST OF WAR

The Allied blockade had not only stopped food getting into Germany. The country was also short of other essential supplies, such as rubber and oil. People had even started wearing clothes made of paper.

The end of the war did not solve this problem suddenly. A peace agreement with Germany was not signed until June 1919. The Allies continued to blockade Germany and Austria up to July 1919. Half-starved children were a common sight in central Europe for some time afterwards.

There was no shortage of statistics, either. Once war was over, people began to count the cost. These two pages include some of these statistics. The pictures have been deliberately chosen to illustrate the statistics.

A How the army's needs increased.

The BEF, August 1914	The BEF, November 1918
120,000 men	2,360,400 men
40,000 animals	404,000 animals
334 lorries, 133 cars	31,700 lorries, 7,694 cars
300 guns, 63 aircraft	6,437 guns, 1,782 aircraft

B Over 480,000 animals died serving with British forces in the war. This photograph shows horses stampeding after a shell has destroyed a German gun.

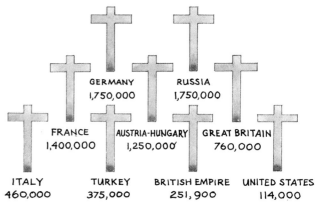

Napoleonic War
1790-1815

Prusso-Austrian War
1866

Franco-Prussian War
1870-71

Balkan War
1912-13

Great War
1914-18

C There were more deaths per day than in any previous war. More British troops were lost in 1918 alone than in the whole of the Second World War.

GERMANY
1,750,000

RUSSIA
1,750,000

FRANCE
1,400,000

AUSTRIA-HUNGARY
1,250,000

GREAT BRITAIN
760,000

ITALY
460,000

TURKEY
375,000

BRITISH EMPIRE
251,900

UNITED STATES
114,000

D Approximate numbers of servicemen who died in the war. About 8 million civilians also died.

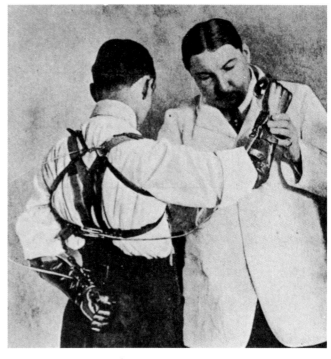

E In addition, about 20 million men were wounded. In Britain alone, 442,000 men never worked again.

F A single square mile of trenches contained the materials shown. By March 1918, the war was costing Britain £6,107,000 a day. (The background picture shows an early British trench.)

Labels on image: 6 million sandbags / 1 million cubic feet of timber / 900 miles of barbed wire

H How imports to Germany dropped. (Figures shown in tons.)

	butter/fats	fish	meat
1916	175,000	420,000	120,000
1917	95,000	150,000	45,000
1918	27,000	80,000	8,000

Le pain KK c'est pour les Boches,
Car pour nous, il est trop moche.

G This French postcard mocked the German food shortage. German wartime bread was called 'K'; 'KK' sounds like 'caca', French for human excrement.

1 a) Look at source D. Why do you think more German troops were killed than British ones?
   b) Why were American losses so small?
2 Why did the war cost so much money? Use as many sources as possible in your answer.
3 a) Which source do you think gives the best idea of the financial cost of the war? Explain how you decided.
   b) Which source do you think gives the best idea of the human cost of the war? Explain how you decided.
4 a) Pick one source which you think may not be reliable. Explain carefully why you have doubts about it.
   b) What can you still learn from your chosen source? Please explain in detail.
5 'Statistics are not as useful as other kinds of sources.' Do you agree with this statement or not? Give detailed reasons.

DEATH BY EXECUTION

Amongst all those who died, a small number were shot by their own side. Many of these deaths were accidental: it was easy for a sentry to make a mistake at night-time if he was nervous. But some of these deaths were deliberate. These included the men who were sentenced to death by court-martial. On average, one British soldier was executed by firing-squad for every week of the war. Their crimes included cowardice and desertion.

Each time, the troops were told at parade time what had happened. But the families were not usually told the truth: they were told that their son had died on active service.

Of course, the army had to keep accurate records and all the details are stored in the Ministry of Defence. They are still secret. The full details will not be released until 2018. However, Parliament was given some details in 1920.

A Sylvia Pankhurst recorded them in *The Home Front* (1932).

> Reports of large numbers of executions at the Front came to us constantly. Men often told us sadly that they had been in firing parties which had been ordered out at dawn to shoot six or seven poor fellows. In 1920, the Under-Secretary of State for War declared that the total number of officers and men sentenced to death from August 1914 to December 1919 was 3076, and that the total death sentences carried out numbered only 343.

B Photographs of executions are rare. This blurred shot shows the execution of a French mutineer.

C The execution post at Poperinghe. In the town's military cemetery there are 18 graves of men shot by firing squad.

However, some people thought these figures were wrong. One of them was H V Clarke who had worked at British HQ in France. He claimed to have copied full details from papers he had seen.

D These were the figures which Clarke quoted. They refer to men executed in France.
1914 – 528
1915 – 10,488
1916 – 12,689
1917 – 13,165
1918 – 1,035

Clarke sent these figures to the newspapers but nobody would publish them. In the end, he took them to Sylvia Pankhurst who published a pacifist newspaper, the *Dreadnought*. He offered to show her his records but she decided to publish the figures first.

E This is what she said happened next. (Same source as A.)

> When the *Dreadnought* was published, detectives called at his house. Finding him away from home, [they] left word they would return next day. In panic, he destroyed the greater part of his records, [keeping] only the first page. Then he came back to Fleet Street to look for me. I happened to be out. He left a note for me and returned home. The detectives had called again and had asked for his records. Still more terrified, he destroyed the only remaining page . . . Clarke was undoubtedly a sincere man. If his figures were incorrect, then he was suffering from delusions.

One soldier who was certainly shot was Private Albert Ingham. He had volunteered at the start of the war and served with the Manchester Pals Battalion. In 1916, he was fighting at the Battle of the Somme.

By October, he could not stand any more and deserted with a friend. When they were caught, they were court-martialled and, together, they were executed in December.

Ingham's father was told that his son had 'died of wounds'. When he found out what had really happened, he insisted that the truth should be recorded on his son's headstone: 'shot at dawn'. No other headstone from the war has these words.

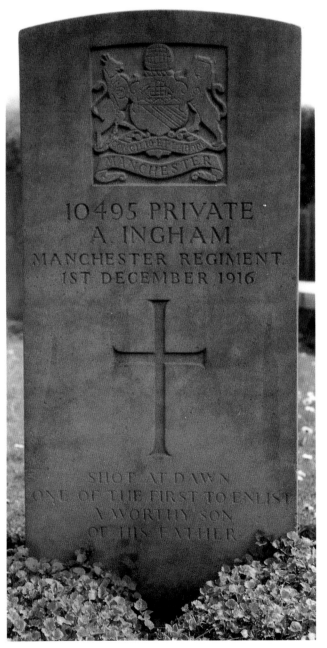

F Private Ingham, aged 24, was 'shot at dawn'.

G This soldier described being in a firing squad.
I think there were 12 of us in the squad and there were 6 or 8 men to be shot. Our rifles were loaded for us and the men were brought out one by one and stood by a post. They all had their hands behind their backs and were blindfolded. There was an officer on one side with a revolver in case a further shot was needed and there was an army chaplain too.

It was an [upsetting] experience. We had been told to aim for the heart. Stretcher bearers took each body away in the short interval between the shooting of each man. When it was all over we were given breakfast. I did not question it. Indeed, I did not question it when an officer shot one of our men who was losing control of himself as we waited an attack. It had to be done for all our sakes.

It was not unusual for an officer to be placed behind the troops. He was armed with a pistol to make sure no one ran away. One man who was wounded on the first day of the Battle of the Somme got back to his own lines. In the trench, he met an armed officer. The officer's job was to shoot anyone who came back unwounded. In an earlier attack in 1914 orders were given that anyone turning back was to be shot or bayonetted.

H Lt Col Hutchison recalled an event during the retreat of 1918. He came across 40 men who were getting ready to surrender.
An action [like] this will in a short time spread like dry rot through an army. It calls for immediate and prompt action. If there [is no] leader of sufficient courage to check it by a word, it must be necessary to check it by shooting. This was done. Of a party of forty men who held up their hands, thirty-eight were shot down with the result that this never occurred again.

---

1 a) Read page 50. How do sources A and D disagree?
b) Write down all the possible reasons why they disagree.
c) Why would a historian be unwise to rely on source D? Give reasons.
d) Does this mean that the figures in source A must be correct? Again, give reasons.
e) What are the strengths and weaknesses of each set of figures?

2 a) Why do you think parents were not told that a son had been executed?
b) Look at source F. Why do you think Private Ingham's father wanted these words on the headstone?

3 a) What opinions are given in source G?
b) How does this writer agree with source H?
c) Do you share their opinions? Give reasons.

L'ÉTERNELLE PETITE GUERRE

" Attaque de front "

A Postcards showed the more relaxed relationships between the sexes.

The British army in 1914 was led by officers who were mostly upper class. At that time, the upper classes did not mix with the working classes. The two groups were almost strangers.

The war changed this. The casualty rate among officers was higher than in the other ranks. As a result, more middle-class people became officers. These officers shared the same trenches with their men; they attacked across No Man's Land together. By 1918, they knew each other better.

Meanwhile, back in Britain, more lasting changes were taking place. Before the war, it was rare for an upper-class or middle-class lady to go out alone. A chaperone accompanied her everywhere. During the war, the lady was out helping in the war effort. Many middle-class women had paid jobs for the first time. Some women even took to wearing trousers. This would have seemed shocking back in 1914.

Attitudes towards sex had changed, too. During the war, many couples decided to live in the present, rather than wait for future happiness. After all, the man might be dead within days of arriving at the front.

In 1914, sex was rarely talked about. In contrast, newspapers during the war received a great many letters about venereal disease. In 1917, troops were issued with condoms and it became easier to buy them in Britain. Even so, illegitimate births rose by 30 per cent.

The new freedom did not end with sex. Women drank, smoked and swore in public. They wore make-up: lipstick first appeared in 1915. Thirty years earlier, this sort of behaviour would have ruined a respectable woman's reputation.

The new freedom was seen everywhere on Armistice Night. The war was over and people wished to celebrate. In many towns, the police were told not to interfere unless there was a risk of someone being killed.

So Britain enjoyed itself. Complete strangers made love in shop doorways and parks. In Trafalgar Square, the crowd demolished a watchman's hut and burned it. The marks on the stonework around Nelson's Column can still be seen today. The war was over and people wanted to forget about it; it was an attitude which lasted for the next decade.

THE BROWN FAMILY'S FOUR WAR CHRISTMASES.

B This cartoon appeared in the *Sunday Pictorial*, 23 December 1917.

VICTORY DAY IN CAMBRIDGE.

C Painting of Cambridge people celebrating the Armistice.

D A report in the *Daily Mail* (17 April 1916).
The wartime business girl is to be seen any night dining out alone or with a friend in the restaurants in London. Formerly, she would never have had her evening meal in town unless in the company of a man friend. But now, with money and without men, she is more and more beginning to dine out.

Most often they are in couples, though [often] one sees merry groups of three or four. After a modest dinner, cigarettes follow, and then there is talk of typing, 'governors', theatres and dress. Very often girls look in for only a cup of coffee, with a cigarette.

E Harold Macmillan, a young officer, wrote to his mother in 1915.
Of all the war, I think the most interesting experience is the knowledge one gets of the poorer classes. They have big hearts, these soldiers.

F Robert Roberts described how working-class life changed in *The Classic Slum* (1971).
Wives no longer talked about 'my boss' or 'my master'. Master had gone to war and Missis ruled the household, or he worked close to her in a factory, earning little more than she did herself.

Historians study changes in the past. They look for different kinds of changes. For instance, the changes described on these pages are mostly social changes. Then, they ask whether these changes have brought progress or not.

1. a) List all the changes which are described on these pages.
   b) Pick any two of these changes and explain why they happened.
   c) Which of these changes do you think the older generation would have disapproved of? Explain how you decided.
   d) In your view, did these changes bring progress? Give careful reasons.

2. a) Study source B carefully. How did life change for each of these people?
   b) What else has changed in the scene?
   c) How and why did life change for the lady of the household?
   d) Do you think she thought this change was progress? Explain your answer.
   e) Do you think this change was progress? Explain your answer.

3. Study the sources carefully. What evidence can you find of economic change? Explain your decision.

1914	1915	1916	1917	1918	1919

The two main parties in British politics in 1914 were the Conservatives and the Liberals. In the 1910 election, they were neck and neck. Labour was then a fairly new party and trailed in third place.

The Liberals were in power when war broke out but the two main parties put their disagreements to one side and co-operated. Almost all MPs supported the war. In fact, by January 1915, 184 MPs had actually joined the forces; they rarely appeared at Westminster.

At first, Parliament had surprisingly little to do with the war. In the first nine months, the Prime Minister, Herbert Asquith, only once told Parliament how it was going. Even then, the issue was not discussed.

B Lloyd George trying his hand at potato spraying in 1917.

A Sir Edward Grey was British Foreign Secretary at the start of the war. This German cartoon called him a 'warmonger and mass-murderer'.

The Liberal Party had a laissez-faire approach to running the country. This meant that they believed in interfering as little as possible. It soon became clear that this was not a suitable way to run the war.

The crunch came in May 1915 when it was clear that the army was short of shells. Asquith invited the Conservatives to join his government and form a coalition . He also made one Labour MP a minister. In July, a new Ministry of Munitions was set up, led by the Liberal David Lloyd George.

None of this made Asquith any better as a wartime leader. In December 1916, the Conservatives forced him to resign and Lloyd George became Prime Minister. It caused a split in the Liberal Party from which it never recovered.

In Britain, we normally have a General Election every five years. This should have happened in 1915 but, because of the war, the government put it off. The election was finally held in 1918.

Lloyd George wanted the coalition to continue after the 1918 election. Asquith disagreed and led a separate Liberal Party; the Labour Party also decided to fight the election on its own.

C A historic moment: women over 30 voted for the first time in the 1918 election.

The coalition won the election and Lloyd George became Prime Minister again – but his government was mostly made up of Conservatives. He hung onto power until 1922 when they forced him to resign.

In the General Election of that year, the Conservatives won a sweeping victory. Labour was the second biggest party: it had more MPs than Asquith's Liberals and Lloyd George's Liberals put together.

Although the two Liberal groups made up their differences by 1923, it was too late. The Labour Party was now properly organised; it had, in effect, become the opposition. The Liberals never again formed a government.

D How the government's power increased from 1914 to 1918. The national debt is the money which Britain owed abroad.

TO-DAY-UNEMPLOYED

PUBLISHED BY THE LABOUR PARTY 33 Eccleston Square, London. S.W. & printed by VINCENT BROOKS DAY & SON LT⁰ 48 Parker St. Kingsway London WC₂

E A Labour Party poster from 1923. This was one of two posters. The first one said 'Yesterday - the trenches.' The war was still an issue, 5 years after it had ended.

1 Please answer in complete sentences.
   a) Why did the parties forget their disagreements when war started?
   b) Why was a laissez-faire policy not suitable in wartime?
   c) Why did the Liberal Party split?
2 a) Which of the four pictures do you think are propaganda? For each one you choose, explain how you decided.
   b) For each one you choose, explain what a historian can learn from it.
3 Design a poster which Lloyd George could have used after the war to persuade people to vote for him. Before you start, think of what his government had done for the country.

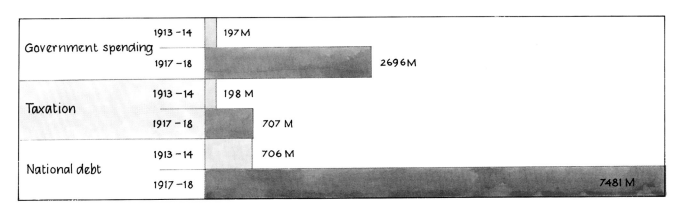

	1913 –14	197 M
Government spending	1917 –18	2696M
Taxation	1913 –14	198 M
	1917 –18	707 M
National debt	1913 –14	706 M
	1917 –18	7481 M

In June 1914, British politicians had been more worried about Ireland than the risk of a European war. In fact, Asquith said the crisis caused by the Archduke's death was 'a good thing'; it would take people's minds off Ireland.

The Irish had been demanding independence since the middle of the 19th century. In 1912, the Liberals had finally passed an Act to give them Home Rule. But this was delayed when war broke out.

One group was annoyed with this decision. It was the Irish Republican Brotherhood (IRB). This was a small secret society, determined to gain independence for Ireland. Its members decided that there had to be a revolt while Britain was busy fighting Germany.

So an uprising was planned for Easter Week in 1916. The plan was that a German ship should bring arms to Ireland and the rebels would capture Dublin. It all went badly wrong.

A The Irish were encouraged to recruit but many saw it as England's war, not Ireland's. When conscription was introduced in 1916, the Irish were not forced to join up.

B The Citizens' Army paraded outside Liberty Hall in Dublin.

The British knew all about these plans. A British patrol boat intercepted the German ship so the arms never got through. An Ulster Protestant, Sir Roger Casement, had arranged for the German help. A German submarine brought him back to Ireland and he was immediately arrested.

The Irish leaders were split. One group tried to call off the uprising. Boys on bicycles rode round Ireland, telling people that it was cancelled. It was even announced in the Sunday papers that there would be no revolt!

Most of the IRB had different ideas. Without the German arms, the revolt stood no chance. 'I shall be shot, swept away, and my colleagues like me,' said Patrick Pearse, one of the leaders. Yet they went ahead.

On Easter Monday, the 2,000 men and women of the Citizens' Army took over key positions in Dublin; they announced that Ireland was free. Within two days, the British outnumbered them by 20 to one. The British plan was to crush the rebels quickly and that is what they did.

By the following Sunday, it was all over. Large areas of Dublin had been destroyed. The British had about 500 casualties; the Irish had about 1,000, including many civilians caught in the crossfire. The rebels were marched across Dublin to await trial. Crowds of Irish booed them on their way.

It was a complete defeat. But what the British government did next played right into the rebels' hands. The leaders were secretly court-martialled and shot. They included James Connolly who had been injured by a sniper's bullet. Unable to walk, he was shot seated in a chair. Source C shows the plaque which records these executions in Dublin's Kilmainham Gaol. Sir Roger Casement was later executed in London.

Reaction was immediate. American newspapers accused the British of revenge. The British Embassy told London that American feeling towards England was at a new low. Many Irish felt the same way.

Too late, the British government tried to make amends. It released most of those arrested after the rising. They went home and began planning a new rebellion. This time, Americans provided money to make sure it would succeed.

The seeds of the future history of Ireland had been sown. Leadership of the Irish republicans fell into the hands of a political party called Sinn Fein. In the 1918 election, they won most of the Irish seats in the British Parliament. But they refused to attend: they set up their own in Ireland instead.

Meanwhile, the Easter week fighters were busy organising a new guerrilla movement: the rebels now called themselves the Irish Republican Army (IRA). In January 1919, shots rang out again in County Tipperary: a new fight had begun.

Sinn Fein

D G K Tull and P Bulwar: *Britain and the World in the Twentieth Century* (1966).
During the war the Sinn Fein Party was formed in Southern Ireland to break with England and set up an independent Ireland.

E Alan Palmer: *Dictionary of Twentieth-Century History* (1979).
Sinn Fein [was] founded in 1902 by Arthur Griffith.

F L C B Seaman: *Post-Victorian Britain* (1966).
Power in Ireland passed into the hands of a minority dominated by Sinn Fein, a group founded by Arthur Griffith in 1904.

G Désirée Edwards-Rees: *Ireland's Story* (1967).
In 1905 Arthur Griffith had founded a society called *Sinn Féin*. The name, meaning 'We Ourselves' [is] sometimes rendered 'Ourselves Alone'.

Working out what caused events in history is never easy. The causes are often linked together, rather like a spider's web. An action may be seen by one group as a consequence of an earlier event: another group may see it as a cause of what happens next.

1 What caused these events:
   a) A delay in starting Home Rule;
   b) The IRB planned a revolt;
   c) The rebels were short of weapons;
   d) Anti-British feeling in America?
2 a) How do sources D, E, F and G disagree?
   b) Is it possible that all these sources are correct? Explain your answer.
   c) How is it possible for sources to disagree like this?
3 a) Look at source B. Why do you think the poster said that they did not serve the Kaiser?
   b) The British called them 'rebels' and the Irish called them 'patriots'. How does this photograph support each view?
   c) The text on these two pages calls them 'rebels'. Does that mean it is biased? Explain your answer.
4 Please write not less than a page to answer this question. What caused the IRA to come into existence?

A The new map of Europe. Nine new countries were created. Three disappeared: they were Austria-Hungary, Montenegro and Serbia.

In January 1919, officials of over 30 countries met in Paris to draw up a peace treaty. The Germans were not invited. In effect, three men made all the decisions. They were President Woodrow Wilson (United States), Georges Clemenceau (France) and Lloyd George (Great Britain).

The three men had different aims. The French wanted to punish Germany and make it pay for the damage it had done in France. Lloyd George knew that many Britons felt the same way. But he was worried that a harsh agreement would make Germany want revenge.

Wilson had his own plan. In January 1918, he had drawn up Fourteen Points which he thought would ensure peace. They included cutting down on arms and setting up a League of Nations to keep the peace in future. He also believed in self-determination – in other words, smaller nations should be independent, if they wished. Britain and France disagreed: they wished to add German colonies to their empires.

The result was a compromise. Germany lost about 13 per cent of its European land and all of its colonies. Germans were very bitter about the agreement. The German government refused to sign it and resigned. But Germany had no real choice. Eventually, the agreement was signed at Versailles on 28 June 1919 – exactly five years after the murder at Sarajevo.

Other treaties were signed in 1919 and 1920 with the other defeated countries. Turkey and Bulgaria each lost land and had their armed forces reduced.

B Some of the terms of the Treaty of Versailles.

1 Germany blamed for starting the war.

2 Land given to Poland and Denmark.

3 Alsace and Lorraine returned to France.

4 All colonies taken away.

5 Reparations to pay for damage.

6 Army cut to 100,000 men.

7 No submarines, **tanks** or aeroplanes

PEACE AND FUTURE CANNON FODDER

The Tiger: "Curious! I seem to hear a child weeping!"

C This famous cartoon of 1919 shows the key figures at the peace conference. From left to right: Lloyd George, Orlando (Italy), Clemenceau and Wilson.

Attitudes to the Treaty

D Marshal Foch, Allied commander.
This is not peace. It is an armistice for twenty years.

E From a German newspaper, June 1919.
Today in [Versailles], the disgraceful Treaty is being signed. Do not forget it. The German people will press forward to reconquer the place among nations to which it is entitled. Then will come vengeance for the shame of 1919.

F Martin Walker: *Daily Sketches* (1978).
[The] most important mistake was to insist that a defeated Germany repaid the allies for the costs of the war. It meant that Germany had to become a rich nation to raise such vast sums. But a prosperous nation was a strong nation, capable of military strength which would allow Germany to mock the demands. Much of the history of the 1920s could be traced to this [basic] stupidity.

G Adolf Hitler said what he thought of the treaty in *Mein Kampf* (1930).
It had all been in vain, then. In vain the death of the two million who gave their lives in the midst of these sufferings. I knew that all was lost. Only fools could place their hope in the enemies' mercy, fools – or liars and criminals. My hatred grew, hatred for those responsible for this deed.

In the days that followed, I became aware of what my fate was to be. I decided to go into politics.

H Propellers into firewood: German aeroplanes were cut up.

1 a) Compare source A with a modern atlas. What changes have happened since 1919?
   b) Write down the names of any three countries whose boundaries have not changed since 1919.
2 a) Why is the child weeping in source C?
   b) Think carefully. Who does the child represent?
   c) What point is the artist making?
   d) Which of the written sources makes the same point? Explain how you decided.
   e) 'Source C is only a cartoon, so it does not really tell a historian anything.' Do you agree? Give reasons.
3 a) 'The Treaty of Versailles was a mistake.' Do the written sources support this statement? Please answer in detail.
   b) 'Did the Treaty of Versailles help to cause the Second World War?' Which sources are most useful in answering this question? Explain how you chose them.

A A British postcard praising the war effort of Indian troops.

Black Africans had their own name for the Great War. They called it 'the war of the white tribes'. Yet many men from the colonies fought with the British. At the end of 1914, 25 per cent of British divisions in France were made up of Indian troops.

Britain held its official victory celebrations in July 1919. She had fought the war partly to stop Germany from taking over her empire. So, that summer, people from all the colonies marched through the streets of London. The great British Empire was on show. In fact, an era was ending.

Earlier that year, Indians had demonstrated for their independence at the Punjab town of Amritsar; British troops shot 379 of them and wounded another 1,200. It was a warning of what was to come: dusk was falling on the British Empire 'over which the sun never set'.

Meanwhile, British troops came home from the war. By the summer of 1919, 80 per cent were civilians once more. At first, most were pleased to be home, even if they could not find a job. Anything was better than fighting in the trenches.

Lloyd George had promised that he would build 'a land fit for heroes to live in'. At first, it seemed as if he would succeed. Trade did well in 1919 and 1920. Wages rose and almost everyone had a job.

Lloyd George had promised to sweep away the slums and build 'homes fit for heroes'. And some new houses *were* built.

But it was not to last. High employment and extra wages meant that people had money to spend – and the price of goods rose. Even bread went up by 60 per cent. By 1921, over 2 million people were unemployed. They included 20 per cent of British builders, who were supposed to be building homes for heroes.

The government tried to bring things under control. It made hefty cuts in its own spending. The house-building programme suffered. And public employees had their pay cut: they included teachers, the police and the army. Ex-soldiers even found their war pensions reduced.

None of this helped to reduce unemployment. It stayed high right through the 1920s and 1930s. People had to wait for another world war to create jobs.

B The Cenotaph in London is the nation's war memorial. Unveiled in 1920, it replaced a temporary wooden one put up in 1919.

WISHING YOU A JOLLY XMAS.

CHEERIO

WE ARE ALL BACK AT OUR OLD JOB.

C A postwar card.

D George Coppard described some events after the war in *With a Machine Gun to Cambrai* (1980).

Lloyd George and company had been full of big talk about making the country fit for heroes to live in, but it was just so much hot air. It was a common sight in London to see ex-officers with barrel organs, [trying] to earn a living as beggars. There were no jobs for the 'heroes' who haunted the billiard halls as I did. The government never kept their promise.

The government [fixed] enormous sums as [gifts] to the high-ranking officers who had won the war for them. Sir Douglas Haig received a tax-free golden handshake of £100,000 (a colossal sum then), an earldom and, I believe, an estate to go with it. If any reader should ask, 'What did the Tommy think about all this?' I can only say, 'Well, what do *you* think?'

E This is what a docker said at the time:

'Fit for 'eroes to live in' – that's wot they told us affore we was let out from that bloody war, and there's me out of work for months and months.

F George Morgan fought in the Battle of the Somme. In 1976, he said:

The best of our generation died there. That's why the country hasn't been the same since. One memory that has never left me is the thought of so many wonderful men being killed. It was such a waste of young manhood.

G John Grout gave his view in *Akenfield* by Ronald Blythe (1969).

I wasn't called up. Nothing happened to me and I didn't remind them. We didn't really miss the men who didn't come back. The village stayed the same.

---

1. a) What impression of postwar life do you get from source C?
   b) What impression of postwar life do you get from sources D and E?
   c) Which impression do you think is more reliable? Give reasons.

2. a) Read sources F and G. How do they disagree?
   b) Does this mean that one of them must be wrong? Give reasons.
   c) Suggest a reason why they disagree.

3. a) What did George Coppard (source D) feel about postwar life? Quote from the source in your answer.
   b) How is his account influenced by his personal circumstances? Please give examples.

4. a) What were the feelings of the speakers in sources E, F and G? Quote from the sources in your answer.
   b) How were their feelings caused by their personal circumstances? Explain your answer.

CHANGE AND CONTINUITY

A *Oppy Wood*, a painting by John Nash (1918). There is still so much live ammunition in this wood that it is closed to the public.

Writers often say that the world was not the same place after the Great War. However, as you might guess, it's not as simple as that. For instance, upper and lower classes had come together in the trenches; they had lived together for the first time in history. But, after the war, the rich returned to their mansions and life carried on much as before. Many of the women who lost their jobs in 1919 went back to working as servants.

On the other hand, football matches started again and the working classes were soon back on the terraces. Matches had stopped in 1915 so that pitches could be used as parade grounds.

In the meantime, going to the cinema had become popular. The war had made it harder for Europeans to make films and American film-makers saw their chance. From then onwards, Hollywood made most of the world's movies.

Other wartime changes were kept in peace time. There were so many widows that women stopped wearing all black clothes. They wore armbands instead. The custom of full mourning never returned.

On the international scene there were huge and lasting changes. In 1914, the world had been dominated by great empires. By 1920, the German, Austro-Hungarian and Turkish empires had been destroyed. In Russia, the emperor was dead and the communists had taken over.

Britain's king had become the world's only surviving emperor. But even he had changed his name. The family name of Saxe-Coburg-Gotha was German: it did not sound right at a time when Britain was fighting the Germans. So, in 1917, George V changed it to 'Windsor', the name still used today.

Of the great empires, only Britain's remained. But Britain had been weakened by the cost of the war: the country's debts in 1919 were 10 times what they had been in 1914. Britain was on the way to becoming a second-rate power. Meanwhile, the United States had become the most powerful country in the world.

The peace settlement had really settled very little. Germans were bitter about the Treaty of Versailles and wanted it changed; no one was more determined than an Austrian named Adolf Hitler.

EGGS AND CHIPS BECAME POPULAR (STEAK WAS SO EXPENSIVE)

CIGARETTES

R.A.F. (FORMED IN 1918)

BRITISH SUMMER TIME

WRIST WATCHES

SHORTER PUB OPENING HOURS

LIPSTICK

B Lasting changes from the Great War. Both wrist watches and cigarettes first became popular in the trenches.

C All quiet on the western front. The remains of Montdidier, in the Somme, seven months after the war ended.

There were lasting changes in the family lives of most ordinary people. Five million of them had fought in the Great War. Few families had not lost a loved one. The Great War cast a shadow over the rest of their lives.

The same was true of the soldiers who survived. Many never settled down in civilian life. One man who had fought at the Somme always stayed at home on each 1 July. The effect of being gassed contributed to some ex-soldiers' deaths 50 years later.

Perhaps we might end this book where we began it – with propaganda. British propaganda had told many lies during the war and the newspapers had printed them all. Not surprisingly, people stopped trusting the newspapers.

This had one tragic consequence. In the Second World War, stories appeared about the German concentration camps and the horrific things that went on there. People didn't believe a word of it. After all, they said, governments told lies like that in the Great War. Too late, it was found that the stories were true, after all.

<u>1</u> a) List the changes mentioned on these two pages.
b) Look at your list. Write out those which were short-term changes.
c) Which of the long-term changes do you think was most important? Give reasons.
d) What different *kinds* of change are in your list?

<u>2</u> a) Make a collection of objects connected with the Great War. If they are valuable, perhaps you could take photographs or make photocopies.
b) Work in pairs. What can you learn about the war from your sources?
c) Which kind of source tells you most about
(i) what the fighting was like and (ii) what life was like during the war? Explain how you decided.

GLOSSARY

abattoir – place for killing animals
abdicated – gave up the throne
alliance – agreement between countries
Allied – on the side fighting the Germans
arbitration – settlement of a dispute by an outsider
armistice – temporary peace
artillery – cannon
attaché – person working at an embassy
attrition – wearing down an enemy
barrage balloon – barrier made of gas-filled balloons
battery – set of big guns
billet – place where a soldier stays
blockade – control of ships entering port
censor – edit
chaperone – female who accompanies a lady in public
civilian – person who is not in the armed forces
clog – shoe with a wooden sole
coalition – alliance of political parties
communiqué – official announcement
desolate – barren; unfit to live in
dug-out – shelter dug in a trench bank
economic – to do with money
guerrilla – fighter in a small group which harasses an army
khaki – dull yellowish-brown (from an Urdu word meaning *dusty*)
kibosh – put the kibosh on = finally got rid of
laissez-faire – policy of not interfering

latrine – toilet
loathsome – disgusting
mobilised – prepared for war
morale – courage, confidence and enthusiasm
munitions – military supplies
mutinies – rebellions against superior officers
neutral – not supporting either side
offensive – attacking
productivity – rate of production
Quaker – member of a pacifist Christian group
quota –share
rationing – sharing out limited amounts
ravenous – very hungry
recession – decline in trade
reconnaissance – surveying
relief – help from public funds
republican – person who does not want a monarch to rule their country
reservist – member of a reserve force
sap – trench leading towards the enemy
serum – liquid used to prevent a disease
shrapnel – piece from a shell
skites – darts obliquely
sniper – soldier who picks off individuals by rifle-fire
strafe – bombardment
synchronise – time to operate together
tribunal – court
U-boat – German submarine (*unterseeboot*)
ultimatum – final demand, including a threat of what will happen if it is not met
unbecoming – not proper
venereal disease – sexually-transmitted disease